"By integrating a variety of mod(
social-scientific interpretation for
phenomena from the biblical wor
explores the historical and cultur;
and his coworkers as change ager, ... groups.
Malina offers a portrait of Timothy, Paul's coworker, which is not
only fully embedded in that world but also opens up fascinating
insights for the modern reader about one of the unsung heroes of the
second-generation Jesus followers."

—*Professor P. F. Craffert*
Chair of the Department of New Testament
University of South Africa, Pretoria

"'A string of pearls' describes Malina's *Timothy*. Although he has no
more data than others, he is able to see those data with satisfying
insight. When Malina focuses a cultural microscope on what is said
about Timothy, he sees pearls of interpretation, understanding more
valuable than pearls. He is at his best, once more, in introducing new
cultural ways of perceiving and understanding the figure Timothy in
his cultural and social world. Timothy is interesting, but the lenses
used to understand him are magical."

—*Jerome Neyrey, SJ*
Department of Theology
University of Notre Dame

"Timothy, Paul's coworker and cowriter, who often has been left out
of focus by Christian collective memory, comes to a new light in this
exciting book. Using social-scientific models about first-century
Mediterranean persons, together with specific information, Bruce
Malina uncovers one of the most influential individuals in the beginnings of Christianity. Very well written and a delight to read."

—*Santiago Guijarro*
Pontifical University of Salamanca, Spain

"This is a fascinating book to read. It is well written in an engaging style and packed with innovative use and a variety of social science models to unravel the mystery of Timothy, the companion and coworker of Paul. Rather than concentrate on the 'theology' of Paul, Malina places the persons of Paul and Timothy within the context of the first-century Mediterranean world as apostle and change agent. The portrait of Paul's cowriter and coworker that emerges is comprehensive and informative. But Malina goes beyond this to look at the development of the 'Timothy traditions' which were formed first in the collection of Luke-Acts. In this journey Malina offers an informative side trip to examine the notion of forgery in the connection with 2 Thessalonians. The end of the book offers a useful analysis of the final traditions about Paul and Timothy in the New Testament, found in the 'forgeries' of the letter to the Colossians and First and Second Timothy and Titus. In all, highly recommended. A delight to read and informative to the student of the New Testament writings."

—*Ray Hobbs*
Ontario, Canada

Paul's Social Network: Brothers and Sisters in Faith
Bruce J. Malina, Series Editor

Timothy

Paul's Closest Associate

Bruce J. Malina

A Michael Glazier Book

LITURGICAL PRESS
Collegeville, Minnesota

www.litpress.org

For the faculty of the Universidad Pontificia de Mexico,
on the 25th anniversary of its reopening.

A Michael Glazier Book published by Liturgical Press

Cover design by Ann Blattner. *Saint Paul*, fresco fragment, Roma, 13th century.

Scripture quotations are from the Revised Standard Version of the Bible, copyright 1952 [2nd edition, 1971] by the Division of Christian Education of the National Council of the Churches of Christ in the United States of America. Used by permission. All rights reserved.

1   2   3   4   5   6   7   8   9

Library of Congress Cataloging-in-Publication Data

Malina, Bruce J.
    Timothy : Paul's closest associate / Bruce J. Malina.
       p.   cm. — (Paul's social network: brothers and sisters in faith)
    "A Michael Glazier Book."
    Includes bibliographical references and index.
    ISBN-13: 978-0-8146-5180-3
       1. Timothy, Saint.   I. Title.

  BS2520.T5M35 2007
  227'.83092—dc22

                                            2007022721

CONTENTS

PREFACE

Human beings are embedded in a set of social relations. A social network is one way of conceiving that set of social relations in terms of a number of persons connected to one another by varying degrees of relatedness. In the early Jesus group documents featuring Paul and coworkers, it takes little effort to envision the apostle's collection of friends and friends of friends that is the Pauline network.

This set of brief books consists of a description of some of the significant persons who constituted the Pauline network. For Christians of the Western tradition, these persons are significant ancestors in faith. While each of them is worth knowing by themselves, it is largely because of their standing within that web of social relations woven about and around Paul that they are of lasting interest. Through this series we hope to come to know those persons in ways befitting their first-century Mediterranean culture.

Bruce J. Malina
Creighton University
Series Editor

INTRODUCTION

Who Is Timothy?

This book is about Timothy. Timothy who? you might ask. This Timothy with no last name lived at a time when most people were known by one name only. When further names were added, it usually meant the person in question was stepping over ingroup boundaries into outgroup territory, where a single name was insufficient. In his hometown and region, Jesus was sufficient to identify the man in his village and in the immediate region. But as he moved past the immediate region, he could be known as Jesus son of Joseph, or in Judea, as Jesus of Nazareth. The same was true of Simon, a follower of Jesus. Jesus gave him a nickname, we are told, and he was called Simon "Rocky" (*petros* in Greek and *kephas* in Aramaic mean "rock"). In wider circles he was also known as Simon son of John.

The one-named Timothy had no further, attested names. Yet he was known in the first Jesus-movement groups from his association with another one-named person, Saul (a Semitic name; Saul also had a "Greek" name, Paul, perhaps because in Greek *saulos* meant "waddler," "one who walked like a prostitute").

This Saul/Paul is well known in modern Christian circles as Paul the Apostle or Paul the Apostle to the Gentiles. And it is through his association with this Paul that the Timothy who forms the subject of this book has become a rather well-known biblical name. (Think of all the "Tims" you know. Most likely they were named after this Timothy.)

This book presents some dimensions of the story of Timothy, associate of Paul the Apostle. Paul is famous in Christian tradition for his letters read in church nearly every Sunday. Churchgoers are used to hearing about the letter of St. Paul to the Thessalonians (one of two), or to the Corinthians (both of these), or to the Galatians, or to the Philippians, or to Philemon, or to the Romans. Historically minded scholars have determined that these seven letters trace back authentically to Paul.

There are other letters traditionally ascribed to Paul (the letter to the Colossians, 2 Thessalonians, Ephesians, 1 Timothy, 2 Timothy, Titus, and even Hebrews), making fourteen in all. But these other letters come from a period after Paul, from people in the third and fourth generation of Christ-believers belonging to groups founded by Paul and his associates. These groups are usually called "churches" (a translation of the Greek word *ekklesia*, meaning "a gathering of people summoned or called together"). Since the word "church" is a very "churchy" word today and might lead the reader to think of buildings and groups of people referred to nowadays as "church," in this book these early gatherings of Christ-believers will be called "Jesus groups."

Paul is famous for founding Jesus groups around the northeast region of the Mediterranean. By the time Paul wrote to the Romans, he believed that he had successfully completed his task to the Gentiles, noting that "from Jerusalem and as far round as Illyricum I have fully preached the gospel of Christ" (Rom 15:19). While it is true that Paul insisted on "thus making it my ambition to preach the gospel, not where Christ has already been named, lest I build on another man's foundation" (Rom 15:20), it is hard to believe that he actually reached all the Gentiles in the region, even though he believed, "I no longer have any room for work in these regions" (Rom 15:23). Consider that the area he is speaking about covers Turkey and Greece and a piece of Yugoslavia, and that Paul lived at a time when travel was essentially by foot on insecure roads or by sea during the months when the sea was passable (March to September). Of course, these regions had different names in the first century AD. They comprised the Roman provinces of Galatia, Asia Minor, Macedonia, Achaia, Mysia, and the like.[1] And while it is hard to believe that Paul actually reached all the Gentiles in those regions, it is equally possible, if not totally probable, that what Paul meant by being an apostle "to the Gentiles" meant something completely different from what that phrase usually means today.

The word "Gentile" is a transcription of sorts of the Latin *gentes*, a word that the famous Bible translator, Saint Jerome (fifth cent.) used to translate the Greek word *ethne* (singular: *ethnos*). The Greek word had a range of meanings in the first century. The Greek dictionary of Liddell and Scott offers the following meanings: company, body of men; a race, tribe; a nation, a people, a particular class of men, a caste. To these meanings the dictionary of Greek papyri by Moulton and Milligan adds: province (outgroup, outsiders of city), category (of people), class (of priests), association (of gravediggers), collegium. "Gentiles" (Greek: *ta ethne*) means "peoples," various populations defined by some presumed common genealogy.

As used by Israelite writers in New Testament times, the word is the Israelite ingroup ethnocentric designation for all peoples other than Israel. From the Israelite point of view, the world consisted of Israel and all the rest of humanity. Thus in Paul's usage *ta ethne* means everyone who is not an Israelite. This category is quite demonstrative of ancient Israelite ethnocentric values, values revealed in all New Testament documents. Since in the New Testament the *ethne*, or Gentiles, are contrasted with Israel, in English "Gentile" has come to mean "one of any nation other than the Jewish" (Oxford English Dictionary). While the

Oxford English Dictionary does describe modern English usage, this popular meaning of Gentiles is totally wrong for antiquity and is really not found in the New Testament. It is based on two erroneous presuppositions: first, that there were "nations" in antiquity, and second, that Paul actually was concerned about "nations other than the Jewish."

Be that as it may, to understand who Timothy was and what he was up to in associating with Paul, it might be useful to consider rather briefly what Paul has to say about Timothy. Perhaps the most significant feature to note is that of Paul's authentic letters, only two were composed by Paul alone—and these are the letter to the Romans and the letter to the Galatians. While Paul's letter to the Romans is considered by scholars to be a rather full statement of Paul's theological thinking, in point of practical affairs the letter is about travel arrangements. Paul had never visited Rome, and he knew well that Rome had Jesus groups founded by others. Recall his policy of not wishing to build on another's foundation (Rom 15:20). So he was not going to Rome to proclaim his gospel of God; rather, as he says in that letter, "I hope to see you in passing as I go to Spain, and to be sped on my journey there by you, once I have enjoyed your company for a little" (Rom 15:24). Paul writes so that Roman Christ believers might show him hospitality as he passes through on his way to Spain.

On the other hand, the letter to the Galatians is notable for its rather harsh tone. In that letter Paul gets as up close and personal as a first-century Mediterranean person can. He omits the usual introductory blessing, accuses the Galatians of being hexed by an evil eye, and generally argues against a range of behaviors adopted by the Galatians, behaviors that went against the innovation that Paul had introduced among them.

The point is that the only documents among the authentic writings of Paul that he alone composed are the letter to the Romans and the letter to the Galatians. All the other letters have co-senders and collaborators. Consider the lineup, in more or less historical sequence:

1 Thess 1:1 Paul, Silvanus, and Timothy, To the church of the Thessalonians in God the Father and the Lord Jesus Christ: Grace to you and peace.

1 Cor 1:1 Paul, called by the will of God to be an apostle of Christ Jesus, and our brother Sosthenes,

2 Cor 1:1 Paul, an apostle of Christ Jesus by the will of God, and Timothy our brother. To the church of God which is at Corinth, with all the saints who are in the whole of Achaia:

Phil 1:1 Paul and Timothy, servants of Christ Jesus, To all the saints in Christ Jesus who are at Philippi, with the bishops and deacons:

Phlm 1:1 Paul, a prisoner for Christ Jesus, and Timothy our brother, To Philemon our beloved fellow worker.

Aside from the first letter to the Corinthians, Timothy is a co-sender and collaborator of all the rest of the letters. One might ask whether the mention of Timothy (and Silvanus in the letter to the Thessalonians, and Sosthenes in the letter to the Corinthians) is a mere formality, or are these early Jesus-group members as responsible for composing those letters as Paul is? If these mentions are a mere formality, Paul could just as well include Timothy, Silvanus, and Sosthenes at the end of the letter, which he reserves for greetings from people in his entourage (see, for example Romans, where Timothy is mentioned). And if these personages are truly fellow writers and collaborators, what would that mean?

While neither Timothy nor Paul were individualistic, like people in our contemporary individualistic society, yet perhaps our experience of collaboration on a book might indicate something of that relationship. As a person who has collaborated in writing a number of books (with Jerome H. Neyrey, Richard L. Rohrbaugh, John J. Pilch), I am convinced that what it takes to realize a collaborated work is mutual trust. It is this trust that allows the collaboration process to proceed to realization, for collaborators must necessarily engage in reciprocal rewriting and editing one another's words and ideas. A successfully collaborative work has no seams; a reader cannot tell where one writer leaves off and another begins. Rather the work reads like the work of a single person.

However, the experience of collaboration that I speak of has been realized in our individualistic culture, where "standing on one's own two feet" is the cultural norm. We even speak of "authors" who express their own views while "authoring." Such was not the case in antiquity. Furthermore, our coauthoring requires whittling down individualistic norms in favor of mutual and rather selfless cooperation. Yet in the end our coauthoring is the melding of two individualistic persons. Not so in antiquity. Collaborators in the past were collectivistic persons. Their cultural norm would move them to focus on supporting the group that they represented (notice that the writers to the Corinthians speak of the practice of "the churches of God" [1 Cor 11:16], and "all the churches" as setting the norm [1 Cor 7:17; 14:33]). Group integrity was their major concern.

In the case of Timothy and Paul (and Silvanus and Sosthenes), the groups in question were the Jesus groups that they had founded, to which they belonged, and whose welfare was their priority. While their letters were successful feats of collaboration, given that their works have no seams, it was not mutual trust that produced that effect so much as mutual and reciprocal devotedness to the collectivity, the Jesus groups which they had founded and of which they were a part. This point will become clear when we consider what sort of person Timothy (and Paul) was in a later chapter.

In any event, while modern successful coauthoring produces a single, unified work of two (or more) individualistic persons, ancient collaboration produced a single, unified work of a group realized by two (or more) collectivistic persons. Just as the folk are ultimately responsible for folksongs, although one or two individuals in the group actually compose those songs, the same is true of the collaborative letters of Paul and Timothy. They are not only to the Thessalonians or Corinthians or Philippians, but they are the collective work of the Thessalonians or Corinthians or Philippians. Their authority comes from their reception by the Jesus group to whom they were written and by whom they were preserved.

Christianity today exists thanks to a number of our Jesus-group ancestors in faith. While these ancestors in faith do include Paul and Timothy and Silvanus and Sosthenes, more importantly they include the people who made up the Jesus groups of Thessalonians and Corinthians and Philippians and Galatians. They were responsible for the articulation of the faith in the letters addressed to them, while Paul and his co-senders composed their letters. I think collectivistic Paul and Timothy and Silvanus and Sosthenes would be very happy with this formulation of their activity as writers. Composing these letters was part of Paul's activity. Timothy, Silvanus, and Sosthenes were part and parcel of this activity. Yet Timothy and Silvanus stand out for being remembered in the fourth-generation document called the Acts of the Apostles, and Timothy and Titus are hallowed in the Pauline tradition for having letters addressed to them by some anonymous third Pauline-generation writer and his group of Christ believers.

In this book, chapter 1 looks at what sort of person Timothy was. Modern biography was born in the Romantic period (nineteenth century), with its concern for the subject, with character development, introspection, and social roles. Biography in this vein is concerned essentially with the psychological development of persons as they face life's trials and deal with them. It is the individual's personality and individual resourcefulness that are of concern as the person in question finds success and/or failure. Such was not the case in antiquity. Persons in antiquity were anti-introspective and not psychologically minded at all. What counted was what went on on the outside of a person, and it was outside, personal forces, human and non-human, that were of the greatest interest. While ancient persons were certainly individuals, they were not individualistic; rather they were collectivistic persons, concerned more with group integrity than with standing on their own to find success. Timothy and Paul were such collectivistic persons, and their letters reveal as much.

Chapter 2 offers a further social-scientific description of how groups develop over time to serve as a foundation for understanding where Timothy fits into the Jesus tradition. This understanding will explain how Jesus groups developed from the first generation of those who actually experienced Jesus through the second generation of Jesus-group members, which included Paul and Timothy. Next followed a third Jesus-group generation, during which the Gospels of Matthew, Mark, and John were written. One letter ascribed to Paul, Silvanus, and Timothy belongs with this generation (2 Thessalonians). Finally, a fourth Jesus-group generation is marked by a broad story running from Jesus to Paul in the documents called Luke-Acts, the letter to the Colossians, and the general letters now labeled to the Ephesians and to the Hebrews, as well as the directives called 1 and 2 Timothy and Titus. Chapter 2 will consider the significance of these four generations, along with their distinctive concerns about Jesus and his proclamation of the kingdom of God (or heaven).

Since Timothy was a member of that second generation of Jesus groups that were founded by Paul and then assisted Paul in his activities, the third chapter offers an overview of ways of understanding Timothy and how he fit into Paul's project. Information for this task will come from those authentic letters of Paul and his co-senders, along with comparative models that describe ancient Mediterranean persons.

The next four chapters focus specifically on Timothy. Chapter 4 turns to the specific mentions of Timothy in the authentic letters of the Pauline collection. Chapter 5 describes how the subsequent traditions about Timothy begin; chapter 6 looks to memories of Timothy in the generation after his; and chapter 7 considers the final traditions about Timothy in the New Testament, in the fourth generation after Jesus, third-generation documents after Paul and Timothy.

CHAPTER 1

Timothy: The Collectivistic Person

Bible readers and churchgoers generally know that there was a certain Timothy who was a coworker of Paul's and a co-sender of several of the Pauline letters. This Timothy came from a time and place far removed from us modern readers. What sort of person was he that Paul, the famous apostle, considered him a very successful associate in the task of spreading what Paul proclaimed as "good news"? This good news, Paul said, was about an innovation begun by the God of Israel with the raising of Jesus of Nazareth from the dead with a view to a forthcoming Israelite kingdom of God.

For modern Christians, this all sounds like religion. After all, this news was about God and Jesus and the kingdom of God. But such was not the case in the first-century Mediterranean world. This good news was essentially political, like the stuff about the government on TV news. What was so political about God's raising Jesus from the dead? You will have to read the Pauline letters closely. If you do, you will see that it was Israel's God, the God of Abraham, Isaac, and Jacob, who raised Jesus from the dead. Then you will find that this raising of Jesus indicated that the God of Israel would establish a new political system, "the kingdom of God," a phrase that refers to a theocracy (Iran is a theocracy). This meant a radical regime change, in Jerusalem and Judea, for Israelites.

This was Paul's good news. Obviously, it was good news only for Israelites, since it was the God of Israel who took the initiative, both in sending Jesus to fellow Israelites to proclaim a new political order (called "the kingdom of God" or "the kingdom of heaven" in first-century, Israelite terms) and in having Paul spread this news to Israelites fanned out around the Mediterranean. Paul recruited Timothy to help him in the task of letting fellow Israelites know about this forthcoming political order.

This chapter is presented in such a way that as you get to know yourself, you might better get to know Timothy. When Americans ask what sort of person somebody might be, they invariably search for qualities of personality in psychological terms. American biography is heavily psychological, concerned with a person's internal states, private decisions, perseverance in overcoming obstacles that might fill a person with doubt and hesitation. A successful biography describes how a person was able to stand on his or her own two feet, to make it in spite of strong, inwardly felt anxieties and deep feelings of intense apprehension, yet with courage in facing so many obstacles.

All these compelling features are internal to a person, part and parcel of a person's character. They are rooted in an individual's psychological make-up and are of interest to Americans because Americans presume that persons are individualistic and psychologically oriented. A well-known anthropologist once described the American person as ". . . a bounded, unique, more or less integrated motivational and cognitive universe, a dynamic center of awareness, emotion, judgment and action organized into a distinctive whole and set contrastively both against other such wholes and against its social and natural background." To this description, he quickly added: "however incorrigible it may seem to us, it is a rather peculiar idea within the context of the world's cultures."[1]

Actually, individualism and individualistic personality are rare in the modern world. Social psychologists like Harry Triandis[2] and Geert Hofstede[3] claim that only 20 percent or so of the world's population is individualistic (for ongoing and ranging studies verifying the point, see the *Journal of Cross-Cultural Psychology*). Arthur Kleinman, an anthropologist and psychiatrist, claims that this sort of individualistic personality described by Geertz emerged in Europe only in the seventeenth century with the social development and acceptance of a "metaself," an introspective self concerned with thinking about how one thinks about how one thinks. The advent of modern science at about the same time correlated with the disruption of the bio-psycho-spiritual unity of human consciousness that had existed until then. As a result, we have developed an "acquired consciousness," whereby we dissociate self and look at the "subjective" self "objectively." Western culture socializes individuals to develop a metaself, a critical observer that monitors and comments on experience. The metaself stands in the way of unreflected, unmediated experience, which now becomes distanced.[4]

Of course, such a metaself-based way of thinking about oneself did not exist in antiquity. To ask what sort of person Timothy was, we will not find any data in any first-century sources that even hint at what we call individualism or individualistic personality. This does not mean that people were not individuals. After all, people were born one by one, nurtured one by one, and could stand alone. But when it came to who they thought they were and what other people thought of them, no one at the time would answer in terms of our individualism.

Stereotypical Thinking

Anthropologically oriented social psychologists call the opposite pole of individualism collectivism. First-century persons like Timothy and Paul and Jesus were collectivistic personalities. A collectivistic personality is one who needs other persons to know who he or she is. Every person is embedded in another, in a chain of embeddedness, in which the test of interrelatedness is crucial to self-understanding. A person's focus is not on himself or herself, but on the demands and expectations of others, who can grant or withhold acceptance and reputation. In other words, individuals do not act independently.

In a collectivistic world, to act independently would make no sense. To use an example based on our way of naming, consider your last name as truly distinctive. If you were a collectivistic person, everyone would know you, for example, as "Smith of Portland." People would think that all Smiths of Portland share something in common, even if there are many Smiths in Portland. If I get to know one Smith of Portland, I get to know them all. What is unique is family (the Smiths), your village (Portland), your region (western Oregon), your fictive family or association (your club or church)—but never you as an individual. All members of the group are equivalently the same; they all share the same significant characteristics. So if you meet one you meet them all. And you can learn about all of them by meeting one of them (as the Latin proverb cited by Vergil had it: *Ab uno disce omnes*, "From one of them learn about all of them," *Aeneid* 2.65).

People in antiquity were judged by the category or categories to which they belonged. Such thinking is called stereotypical thinking. Of course, it exists today when, for example, people speak of the behavior and outlook of Catholics, Baptists, Democrats, New Yorkers, and the like. But individuals in all of these categories are expected to stand on their own two feet, to work for their own success, to follow their individual conscience—in short, they are to act as individuals, individualistically. The biographies on the Biography Channel are of interest precisely because they describe individuals with their individual characteristics living out their individual stories in the face of all sorts of challenges. While Americans wish to be treated as individuals, they can and do make stereotypical judgments.

Now such stereotypical judgments were normal and expected in antiquity. Consider the point of view expressed in the following statements. Cicero observes how the Carthaginians (from Carthage) are fraudulent and liars because their ports are visited by too many merchants. Then there are the Campanians (the region around Naples), who are so arrogant because of the fertility and beauty of their land. And the Ligurians (from the region around Genoa) are hard and wild because they are just like all other people who struggle to make mountain soil productive (*Agrarian Laws* 2,95, pp. 470–475). Josephus, an Israelite writer, notes how the Tiberians (from Tiberias in Galilee) have "a passion for war" (Josephus, *Life* §352, p. 131); Scythians (from north of Iran) "delight in murdering people and are little better than wild beasts" (Josephus, *Against Apion* §269, p. 401). In "the seamanship of its people . . . the Phoenicians in general have been superior to all peoples of all times" (Strabo, *Geography* 16. 2. 23; VII, p. 269); "this is a trait common to all the Arabian kings," that they do "not care much about public affairs and particularly military affairs" (Strabo, *Geography* 16. 4. 24; VII, p. 357). "These are the marks of the little-minded man. He is small limbed, small and round, dry, with small eyes and a small face, like a Corinthian or Leucadian" (Ps. Aristotle, *Physiognomics* 808a, 30-33, p. 103). And in the New Testament we find judgments such as: "Cretans are always liars, evil beasts, lazy gluttons" (Titus 1:12) and "Can anything good come out of Nazareth?" (John 1:46).[5]

The first-century Mediterranean people did not know one another very well in the way we are expected to know people: psychologically, emotionally, intimately, through personality and character. Nor did they know themselves in these terms. Ancient Mediterraneans depended on others to tell them who they were. Consider Jesus' question in Mediterranean perspective: "Who do people say that I am?" (Mark 8:27). People neither knew nor cared about psychological development; they were not introspective.

High Context and Low Context

What does such normal stereotypical thinking indicate? Stereotypical thinking is typical of "high context" societies. This very valuable insight has been provided by anthropologist Edward

T. Hall.[6] He has called attention to the prevailing "language context" generally in vogue in a society. Hall refers to low-context and high-context societies. Low-context societies produce detailed texts, spelling out as much as conceivably possible, leaving little to the imagination. The general norm is that most things must be clearly set out; hence information must be continually added if meaning is to be constant. Such societies are fine-print societies, societies "of law," in which every dimension of life must be described by legislators to make things "lawful," including detailed legal directions about how much fat is allowed in commercially sold sausage, for example. The *Congressional Record* offers hours of low-context reading for whoever might wish to be entertained in this way. Hall considers the United States and northern European countries as typically low-context societies. This book, too, is an instance of a low-context document. The need to spell out all the general presuppositions involved in understanding another culture or a person from another culture is a low-context trait.

On the other hand, high-context societies produce sketchy and impressionistic texts, leaving much to the reader's or hearer's imagination. Since people believe that few things have to be spelled out, few things are in fact spelled out. People presume, for example, that stereotypes offer rather full understanding of any individual one might meet. In the Mediterranean region, helping out a person in dire need makes that person obligated for the rest of his or her life to the helper (in the Bible paying this obligation is called "having mercy"). No need to spell out all the obligations as we would when we sign for a car loan. There is no need to spell out all the general presuppositions involved in understanding another culture or a person from another culture for high-context people. All Americans are the same. And all Europeans are the same. In high-context societies little new information is necessary for meaning to be constant. Hall lists the Mediterranean, among other areas, as populated with high-context societies. Clearly, the Bible, along with all other writings from ancient Mediterranean peoples, fits this high-context profile.

The typical communication problem in low-context societies such as the United States is giving people information they do not need, hence "talking down" to them by spelling out absolutely everything. Since people in low-context societies are used to low-context documents, in which everything is spelled out, they tend to judge the Bible quite ethnocentrically, as though it were a low-context collection of writings in which everything is, in fact, spelled out. For the vast majority of Americans, the culturally high-context Bible is "obviously" a low-context document that contains all necessary information, adequately spelled out, for human living according to God's will.[7]

Thus most American people believe that the Bible has the answer to all of life's problems for all peoples of all times. However, since the Bible is historically and culturally high context, it does not in fact articulate "everything." Rather, biblical writers presumed that they would have high-context readers who would know exactly what they were talking about and what frames of reference or scenarios the reader would need to use to understand. And twenty-first-century Americans are not those first-century high-context readers. Our information about Timothy, of course, comes from high-context documents that provide full and adequate first-century information about the man and his activities. For later, low-context readers like us, this information seems thin, sparse, and inadequate. Hence our problem: how to retrieve the necessary information to expand what to us are thin and sparse high-context bits of information for an adequate modern understanding. A good first step toward understanding him as a person is to understand collectivistic personality in greater detail.

Since he was a first-century eastern Mediterranean person, we can safely assume that Timothy, like his contemporaries, was enculturated into a collectivistic society and hence was a collectivistic person. He certainly was not an individualistic self.

> The self here is defined as all the statements a person makes that include the word "I," "me," "mine," and "myself." This definition means that all aspects of social motivation are included in the self. Attitudes (e.g. I like . . .), beliefs

(e.g. X has attribute X in my view), intentions (e.g. I plan
to do . . .), norms (my ingroup expects me to do . . .), roles
(my ingroup expects people who hold this position to do
. . .), and values (e.g. I feel that . . . is very important), are
aspects of the self.

The self is coterminous with the body in individualist
cultures and in some of the collectivist cultures. However,
it can be related to a group the way a hand is related to the
person whose hand it is. The latter conception is found in
collectivist cultures, where the self overlaps with a group,
such as family or tribe.[8]

In the *Journal of Cross-Cultural Psychology*, for example, ongoing investigation into social psychological types as matrices
for individual behavior has settled upon a continuum that runs
from individualist to collectivist. Individualism, roughly speaking, means that individual goals precede group goals. Collectivistic means that group goals naturally precede individual
goals. With a view to comparison, what follows begins with a
brief sketch of the individualistic notion of self prevalent in the
United States. One can then compare this individualistic self
with a description of the collectivistic self.

Individualism American Style

The features of individualism should be readily recognizable
by most American readers, since individualism is a feature of
mainstream American society. The reason for describing the
qualities of American individualism here is to enable a U.S.
reader to reflect upon these characteristics that are taken for
granted in our society. And the goal of these reflections is to
underscore the fact that none of these qualities are found in the
ancient Mediterranean. No one in the whole New Testament
shared in such values, as hard to believe as that may be.

To begin with, individualism may be described as the belief that
persons are each and singly an end in themselves, and as such
ought to realize their "self" and cultivate their own judgment,

notwithstanding the push of pervasive social pressures in the direction of conformity. "Be all that you can be." In individualist cultures most people's social behavior is largely determined by personal goals that often only slightly overlap the goals of collectives such as the family, the work group, the tribe, political allies, coreligionists, fellow countrymen, and the state. When a conflict arises between personal and group goals, it is considered acceptable for the individual to place personal goals ahead of collective goals. Thus individualism gives priority to the goals of single persons rather than to group goals. What enables this sort of priority is focus on self-reliance in the sense of independence, separation from others, and personal competence.

For U.S. individualists, freedom from others and self-reliance are important values. Yet the defining attributes of individualism are: distancing of self from ingroups, emotional detachment, and competition. The term "ingroup" here refers to a relatively small group of people, within a wider context, whose common interest tends to exclude others. In 1906 William G. Sumner called attention to the differentiation that arises between ourselves, the we-group (hence ingroup), and everybody else (the others-groups, or outgroups).[9] Individualists can show much emotional detachment from others, extreme lack of attention to the views of others, relatively little concern for family and relatives, and the tendency toward achievement through competition with other individualists.

Individuals do what makes sense to themselves and provides them with satisfaction rather than what must be done as dictated by groups, authorities, parents. While great guilt feelings might be triggered by abandoning the dictates of groups, authorities, and parents, the individualist believes that he or she is above those dictates. The cardinal virtues of individualists include self-reliance, bravery, creativity, solitude, frugality, achievement orientation, competitiveness, concern for human rights, pragmatism, freedom, competence, satisfaction, ambition, courage, and goals such as freedom from limits and personal accomplishment. Success depends upon ability; the outcome of success is achievement.

Other characteristics include sexual activity for personal satisfaction (rather than procreation, unless personally sought); future orientation (but in terms of short-time perspective); emphasis on equal exchange (that is, balanced reciprocity); the use of wealth to change social structures; instrumental mastery (that is, the need to dominate people, things such as the environment, and events); exclusion of persons who are too different. Moreover, there is nearly exclusive emphasis on the nuclear family, with ready geographic mobility, and a presumption of self-reliance and independence. Individual rights and individual privacy have priority.

Consequently, socialization in individualistic cultures looks primarily to what the person can do, to developing an individual's skills, and only secondarily to developing a sense of group identity. Children learn independence first of all. In child-mother relationship, enjoyment and mutual satisfaction (having fun together) are what count. Individualistic socialization results in high scores in self-other differentiation. After parents, concern with peer socialization is common, with a concomitant development of skills in dealing with peers (not with superiors or subordinates). Individualists perhaps never acquire skills to facilitate the smooth functioning of a group. The common good is rarely in focus.

Furthermore, in individualistic societies the individual's sense of insecurity is accompanied by a concomitant large outlay of resources for police and prisons. This feature repeats itself in a national sense of insecurity along with large military expenditures. Such cultures also display prejudice toward racial and religious groups that are too different. Just as individuals frequently entertain unrealistic interpersonal relationships, their society just as frequently engages in unrealistic international relationships, with the significant presence of crime against persons (e.g., sexual crimes, assault), more hospital admissions, more drug abuse, and, of course, more wars than collectivistic societies engage in.

The self in individualist cultures is a bundle of personal attributes. Identity derives from what one has: skills, experiences, accomplishments, achievements, property. Attributes such as being logical, balanced, rational, and fair are considered important. Thus people define themselves by what they do in society, not by their ingroup memberships. Social functions are judged to be individually acquired attributes. So individualists often find the behavior of collectivists in intergroup relations quite "irrational." Individualists are emotionally detached from their ingroups and do not always agree with ingroup policies.

Furthermore, individualists are extremely introspective and highly psychologically minded. Thus individual behavior is presumed to be best explained by internal psychological mechanisms rather than by ingroup norms, goals, and values. They perceive their ingroups as highly heterogeneous, and they experience little sense of a common fate with ingroup members. They do have larger ingroups (for example, the entire United States), but in that context norms are loosely imposed and boundaries are not sharp and clear but are highly permeable.

The social perception of individualists is dominated by what others in some ingroup of significance are doing (not what they are thinking). Individualists belong to many ingroups, each of which controls only a narrow range of behavior (for example, some groups receive only organizational dues). Thus there is weak attachment to ingroups, with conformity to ingroup authorities determined by personal calculation. Compliance can never be taken for granted. Language is low context, that is, the contents of any communication are highly developed, spelled out in detail. In conflict, individualists side with horizontal relations (siblings, friends, equals) over vertical ones (parents, employers, government officials).

Some of the themes distinctive to U.S. individualist literature include: dignity of individual humans, individual self-development, autonomy, privacy, the individual as the basis of society; individuals as used to analyze social phenomena, as the bases of political, economic, religious, or ethical analyses; individuals as the sole locus of knowledge. In fact, it has been demonstrated that U.S. behavioral sciences, evolutionary biology, and economic analyses are biased in favor of the scientists' own individualist culture, with little concern for broader human nature and collectivistic orientations.

The advantages of individualism include freedom to do what one wishes, ability to maximize satisfaction, self-actualization, and creativity, without penalties for not fulfilling undefined duty to the collective, for not doing what the group expects, for not meeting group obligations. In industrialized and information cultures, the advantage of individual action increases independence, creativity, and self-reliance. While individualists pursue an "exciting" life, with a range of varied enjoyment and pleasure, at times such pursuit entails aggressive creativity, conformity, and insecurity.

Thus some of the negative concomitants of individualism include the following. Interpersonal competition is often counterproductive and can lead to distress and aggression. Individualistic competitiveness often leads to extreme concern for status, at times with violence. People in individualist cultures often experience more conflict within their families than people in collectivist cultures. The greater emphasis on achievement in individualist cultures often threatens the self and causes insecurity. Socially, such insecurity in the individual leads to excessive concern about national security and feeds the arms race.

In conclusion, what must be kept in mind is that the individualism experienced by affluent, socially and geographically mobile modern segments of U.S. society dates back only to the rise of U.S. urbanism at the beginning of the twentieth century, when urban agendas gained prominence and agriculture had become the occupation of extremely few. In the minds of most Americans who are individualistic, the social unit of society is not the group, the guild, the tribe, the city but the individual person.

In sum, in the high context, that is, the New Testament documents, there are no persons described with anything that might be called individualistic traits. Neither Jesus nor Peter nor Paul nor Timothy was such an individualist. There simply was no such individualism in New Testament times. Triandis has noted that the individualism that is most important in the United States and northern Europe is of the least importance to the rest of the cultures of the world.[10] Consequently, if we encounter any "self" in the New Testament, it must necessarily be a collectivistic self.

Timothy, the Collectivistic Personality

Nowadays individualism seems totally strange and esoteric, incomprehensible and even vicious, to observers from collectivistic societies. There is little doubt that if Jesus, Paul, or Timothy were to observe U.S. society, they too would find Americans strange, incomprehensible, and uncivilized in many respects. What, then, was it that characterized those collectivists?

Timothy was a collectivistic personality. He shared the belief that the group(s) in which he was embedded was an end in itself, and as such he ought to realize distinctive group values, notwithstanding the weight of his own personal drive in the direction of self-satisfaction. His social behavior was largely determined by group goals that required the pursuit of achievements that improved the position of his group. The defining attributes of his enculturation were the integrity of his family or kin group and the integrity of the larger, extended kin group of which he was made aware, while keeping his primary ingroup in "good health."

The groups in which Timothy was embedded formed ingroups in comparison with other groups. These other groups were outgroups that did not command his allegiance and commitment. Ingroups consisted of persons who shared a common fate, generally rooted in circumstances of birth and place of origin. Such ingroups are said to be ingroups by ascription. A person was born into his ingroups and did not choose them. While individualists belong to very many ingroups, they really have shallow attachment to all of them.

Timothy, on the other hand, was embedded in very few ingroups and was strongly attached to them. These included his extended family in Lystra as well as the Israelite society in that town and neighboring towns, and eventually the Jesus group, an elective association in his local Israelite society. His ingroups in turn controlled a wide range of his behaviors. His behavior toward the ingroup was consistent with what the ingroup expected. But behavior toward everyone else (for example, strangers, non-Israelites, Romans, and the like) was characterized by defiance of authority, competition, resentment of control, formality, rejection, arrogant dogmatism, and rejection of any attempt at influence that had the outgroup as a source.

As a person of good repute, Timothy was greatly concerned with the views, needs, and goals of his ingroup rather than with single group members. With ingroup members, he practiced generalized reciprocity with a sense of obligation, duty, security. The virtues he and his peers shared were traditionalism, harmony, obedience to ingroup authority, equilibrium, always doing what was proper, cooperation, fatalism, pessimism, family centeredness, high need for affiliation, succor, self-abasement to the group, nurturance, acquiescence, dependency, high value in staying within one's rank in a hierarchy.

Timothy and his ingroup peers were enculturated to view marital sexual relations as exclusively for procreation, a fulfillment of social duty. They shared and highly esteemed social virtues and attitudes that looked to the benefits of the group. He had a well-developed sense of shame, filial piety, respect for the social order, self-discipline, concern for social recognition, humility, respect for parents and elders, acceptance of his position in life, and preserving his public image. He valued anything that cemented and supported ingroup interpersonal relations. Of course, he was taught that his primary concern was the security and honor of his ingroup (most often his kin group). Any success in his life was fame that redounded to the group. He shared many common goals with others in his ingroup and engaged in interpersonal relationships with longtime perspective (such as with his mother, siblings, and cousins). Any wealth he might have acquired was used to maintain the social standing of his group.

The social norms and obligations that Timothy followed were defined by his ingroup rather than determined by his own quest for personal satisfaction. He harbored beliefs shared with the rest of his ingroup members rather than beliefs that might distinguish him from the ingroup. And like others in his section of Lystra, he put great stock in readiness to cooperate with other ingroup members. He demonstrated this readiness when he was recruited by Paul as assistant in his change-agent tasks (see pp. 62ff.). Paul's gospel of God and the forthcoming Israelite theocracy provided him with a set of blanket Israelite goals, attitudes, beliefs, or values that superseded any of his own. His ready acceptance indicated that he enjoyed doing what the ingroup and the God of the ingroup expected.

Timothy was socialized to key in on developing habits of obedience, duty, sacrifice for the group, group-oriented tasks, cooperation, favoritism toward the ingroup, acceptance of ingroup authorities, nurturing, sociability, and interdependence. Evidence for this comes from the way Paul assessed Timothy's value in spreading the Israelite innovation that Paul proclaimed. The outcomes of such socialization produced a person with strong emotional attachment to others in the ingroup, with broad concerns for group members and a greater tendency toward ingroup cooperation and group protectiveness. Like Paul, Timothy did what he had to do as dictated by the command of the God of Israel and ingroup demands rather than by what brought personal satisfaction. In the conflicts that arose in his change-agent activity, Timothy unsurprisingly sided with vertical relationships (Paul and other authorities) rather than with horizontal ones (spouse, siblings, friends).

Like Paul, Timothy was a dyadic self, constantly requiring another to know who he was. His was a group self that internalized group perspectives to such an extent that he could respond automatically as ingroup norms specified without doing any sort of utilitarian calculation. This was a sort of "unquestioned attachment" to the ingroup. It included the perception that ingroup norms were universally valid for all Israelites (a form of ethnocentrism) and required automatic obedience to Jesus-group authorities, with a willingness to support the ingroup even in dire circumstances. These characteristics were usually associated with distrust of, and unwillingness to cooperate with, outgroups. As a matter of fact, often outgroups were considered a different species, to be evaluated and treated like a different species of animate being. Jesus groups were the "true Israel" (Gal 6:16).

As a collectivist person, Timothy defined himself to outsiders largely by genealogy, gender, and geography: family and people (civilized Israelites, i.e., Greeks), gender (male) along with place of origin (ultimately Judea), and place of residence (Israelite community in Lystra). These categories sufficed for any and all psychological descriptors. To outgroups, the self is always an aspect or a representative of the ingroup, which consists of genealogically related, gendered persons who come from and live in a certain place. To ingroup members, the self is a bundle of roles, ever rooted in genealogy, gender, and geography. One does not readily distinguish self from one's social role(s). The performance of duties associated with roles is the path to social respect. On the other hand, social perception is seen through the prism of who the other is, that is, to which group(s) the other belongs.

Like other collectivist persons, Timothy was concerned about the results of his actions on and for others in the ingroup. He would readily share material and nonmaterial resources with group members, as his willingness to accompany Paul indicated. He was concerned about how his behavior appeared to others, since he believed that the outcomes of his behavior should correspond with ingroup values. All ingroup members feel involved in the contributions of their fellows and share in their lives. Thus Timothy felt strong emotional attachment to the ingroup, perceiving all group members as relatively homogeneous, with their behavior regulated by group norms, based on acceptance of group authorities with a view to ingroup harmony and achievement at the expense of outgroups.

Why would a person like Timothy, living in the Israelite diaspora, willingly accept Paul's invitation to help him? One good, collectivistic reason is that ingroup members felt responsible for fellow group members and their actions. First-century Israelites felt responsible for fellow Israelites, and upon forming Jesus groups, they felt responsible for fellow Jesus-group members. This has implications for intergroup relations. Specifically, in collectivism one expects solidarity in action toward other groups, including competing Israelite groups. Joint action is the norm. Good outcomes for the other group are undesirable, even when they are in no way related to one's own outcomes. Each individual is responsible for the actions of all other ingroup members, and the ingroup is responsible for the actions of each individual member. Thus, for instance, ancient Israelites related to Romans in response to Roman policies toward the house of Israel as if each Roman were the maker of those policies. The Romans, in turn, interpreted the actions of individual "Judeans" (the Roman name for the members of the house of Israel) as the actions of all Judeans.

What were the features of the collectivist Jesus groups that Paul and Timothy founded? Collectivists evidence high rates of social support when unpleasant life events occur. Based on studies of modern collectivist societies, there is empirical evidence which suggests that very positive social indicators characterize societies in which the ingroup (kin and fictive kin group) is a normative reference group that provides strong social ties, emotional warmth, and prompt penalties for deviance. These features are what Jesus-group "love" was about. These Jesus groups were culturally homogeneous and included active gossip, frequent rites (baptism and the Lord's Supper), ancestral myths and legends (the story of Jesus), a plausible ideology (the theology of the God of Israel), and clear indicators of membership (mutual love).[11]

Quasi-Individualists in Antiquity

Obviously, Timothy, like the rest of the people one meets in the pages of the New Testament, was essentially collectivistic. However, individualistic-like behavior did exist in the collectivist societies of the ancient Mediterranean world, as it does in modern collectivist societies. To begin with, we might note that the collectivist societies of antiquity (and modern ones too) were strongly hierarchical, shaped like a pyramid, with heavy emphasis on the wide variations in vertical social status and rigid social stratification. People were expected to mind their own status and show respect or disrespect for the status of others.

At the extreme top and bottom of the stratification scale, such hierarchies tend to produce pockets of individualistic-like behavior in otherwise collectivist situations. For example, the elite members of otherwise collectivist societies rather quickly become quasi-individualists. They are often motivated by pleasure, narcissism, individual personal needs, or achievement aspirations. Triandis cites Latin America as a contemporary example.[12] There the elite indulge in all kinds of conspicuous consumption, carnivals, trade, luxury goods, and so on. The picture is not at all unlike that in ancient Rome, where a similar quasi-individualism emerged among the urban elite. Although these elite (2 percent or less of the population) were collectivist personalities in several distinctive ways, they differed markedly from the collectivists that predominated elsewhere in the society.

Yet these "individualistic" persons in collectivist societies are not really the equivalent of the introspective, psychologically minded, self-reliant individualists familiar to modern Americans. Rather they are either (1) elite, rather narcissistic, acquisition-oriented, self-indulgent, and competitive persons or (2) rootless, disconnected, socially degraded persons. In both cases these pseudo-individualists display an outlook that derives from the special positions they occupy in a hierarchical social system. Since they share a few of the characteristics of individualists familiar to Americans, they are properly labeled "quasi-individualist" in order to distinguish them from the familiar American social personality pattern.[13]

As just noted, such quasi-individualism can likewise be found at the other end of the ancient (and modern) hierarchy. Those at the bottom included the beggars, prostitutes, disinherited sons, orphans or abandoned children left to fend for themselves. This bottom rank did not include household slaves, since they were often part of a family (the Latin word *familia* includes slaves). In modern terms, such bottom-most people were cut off from the ingroups that guaranteed survival in collectivist cultures. While in modern societies such people are called marginalized, that description would be inappropriate in antiquity, for they were not at the margins of their society but at the bottom. Beggars, orphans, prostitutes, and the like may not have conformed to the norms of the higher strata, but no one in ancient society, not even beggars and prostitutes, lived outside the social norms prescribed for those in their respective positions. Their behavior fit recognizable patterns of those at the bottom-most stratum. Their quasi-individualistic behavior did not come from personal choice; it was forced upon them by their circumstances in life.

In sum, then, though the Mediterranean societies of antiquity were collectivist in outlook, two types of behavior similar in some ways to individualistic behavior existed as well. There was, first, the narcissistic and hedonistic behavior of the urban elite at the top of the hierarchy, and second, the socially cut-off behavior of the degraded and bottom-most. The first was an outlook derived from privilege and choice, the second from isolation and despair. It is important to recognize that both types of quasi-individualistic behavior are present in the New Testament story. In the story of Paul, Timothy, and their companions, these Jesus-group change agents meet with such quasi-individualists in their encounters with elite kings and governors as well as with beggars.

Conclusion

Without having recourse to psychology and psychological analysis, a New Testament reader can usefully apply the features of collectivism to understanding and describing Timothy and his coworkers as well. Such a stereotypical understanding forms a good fit with the culture in which Timothy was born and functioned as an adult. He was undoubtedly initially assessed in collectivistic terms by his contemporaries as well, since, as previously noted, people in collectivistic societies are not introspective. They are simply not psychologically minded. Timothy's general concern was with group integrity, not with standing on his own and pursuing his own purposes. Timothy was enculturated to seek to maintain the integrity of his own collectivistic group, with his specific family located in a specific village, which in turn was located in a specific region, which in its turn was located in a common people (tribe, common collectivity). We can be certain that he saw his society in terms of a Russian-doll or Chinese-box arrangement of his family (parents, brothers and sisters), his village, his region, and his people. And with his acceptance of Paul's gospel of God, Timothy joined another basic fictive family and upon invitation took up the role of change-agent assistant.

However, none of the details required to fill in the specifics of Timothy's ingroup are available from the letters on which he collaborated with Paul or from Paul's description of the tasks Timothy fulfilled. Such details will be forthcoming in our sources only with the third generation of Pauline Jesus-group members, for reasons that will be explained in the following chapter. As previously noted, Timothy was brought up and lived in a high-context society characterized by sketchy and impressionistic conversations and documents, leaving much to the reader's or hearer's imagination and common knowledge.

CHAPTER 2

The Jesus Tradition: Where Does Timothy Fit In?

I n the previous chapter we were concerned with discovering what sort of person Timothy was. The characteristics of collectivist personality describe him rather well. However, since this book is a sort of biography, it is important to know not only who he was but perhaps to determine more specifically when he lived.

This question of dating Timothy (or Jesus or Paul) is usually an activity of great scholarly concern among New Testament interpreters and historians. The reason for this concern is that in the modern understanding of non-contemporary people, a primary step in writing (or understanding) the story of any group or people is to situate them in time, to chronicle data about them.[1] Chronicle as a first step in history writing derives from post-Enlightenment norms for drawing up historical narratives of what really happened. For proper sequencing of events, one has recourse to calendric determinations, that is, in what year or month or on what day did something happen in the past. The real problem, of course, is that in Greco-Roman antiquity until the sixth century AD, there really was no universal calendar. There was no fixed and stable numbered sequence of units, whether of years or months (for Arabs, thanks to Islam, this happened in the seventh century).

In antiquity the main question was: Who were the significant personages around whom some event happened? In other words, the main way of dating was in terms of and in relation to significant persons. For example, in Christian creeds, the date of the death (and resurrection) of Jesus is "under Pontius Pilate." Similarly, the writer of the Gospel of Luke, "the historian," dates the beginning of the story of Jesus by noting Caesar Augustus and Quirinius (or better, Quintilius), governor of Syria (Luke 2:1-2). And the date for the first activity of John the Baptist and Jesus of Nazareth is determined as follows:

> In the fifteenth year of the reign of Tiberius Caesar, Pontius Pilate being governor of Judea, and Herod being tetrarch of Galilee, and his brother Philip tetrarch of the region of Ituraea and Trachonitis, and Lysanias tetrarch of Abilene, in the high-priesthood of Annas and Caiaphas, the word of God came to John the son of Zechariah in the wilderness. (Luke 3:1-2)

We have no such specific significant persons to date Timothy; yet from the Pauline letters we are certain that Timothy was a Jesus-group member. And there is a very valuable way of dating the sequence of Jesus groups. This method might be called a generational approach, in which, again, persons are prominent, not numbers. A generation is marked by new non-contemporary people in a Jesus-group chain. Generations here are not years but chains of people. For Jesus-movement groups, we obviously begin with Jesus and those about him (Peter and the Twelve, their families, their followers); they marked a first generation. A second generation includes Paul and his coworkers, who followed upon the first Jesus generation but did not experience Jesus. There is nothing in the Pauline writings about what Jesus said and did. This second generation likewise included the other non-first-generation persons mentioned in Paul's letters. Given Timothy's connection with Paul, this is where he fits in. He was a second-generation Jesus-group member.

The writers of the Gospels of Matthew and Mark, who give no evidence of having known Paul or Jesus, tell the story of Jesus. Such interest in telling the story of some prominent first-generation person—in this case Jesus—is an indication of third-generation activity, as will be explained shortly.

Finally, there is the anonymous writer of the Gospel of Luke and of the companion volume called the Acts of the Apostles; this writer tells the story of Jesus as well as the story of Peter, Barnabas, Paul, Silvanus, Timothy, and others in the second Jesus-group generation. As the composer of Luke-Acts indicates in the prologue of his Gospel (Luke 1:1-4; see below), he was a fourth-generation Jesus-group member. So what does this tell us?

In place of the usual approximate numeric datings of modern historians, this chapter proposes an explicit social-scientific general principle to explain both why Timothy's generation, including Paul, was not very interested in what Jesus said and did and why there are Gospel stories at all. Consider the principle of third-generation interest, an explanatory device first articulated by the historian Marcus Hansen. Nearly seventy-five years ago Hansen wrote:

> Anyone who has the courage to codify the laws of history must include what can be designated "the principle of third generation interest." The principle is applicable in all fields of historical study. It explains the recurrence of movements that seemingly are dead; it is a factor that should be kept in mind particularly in literary or cultural history; it makes it possible for the present to know something about the future. The theory is derived from the almost universal phenomenon that what the son wishes to forget the grandson wishes to remember. The tendency might be illustrated by a hundred examples.[2]

Hansen's hypothesis was further developed and applied to the United States some fifty years ago by the sociologist Will Herberg.[3]

On the basis of the works of Hansen and Herberg, this principle of third-generation interest might be described as follows. *When a first generation has experienced significant and irreversible change rooted in some appreciable social alteration, in response to this experienced change the second generation seeks to ignore (hence "forget") many dimensions of first-generation experience, while the third generation seeks to remember and recover what the second generation sought to forget.*

As Hansen stated, there really are hundreds of examples of this process, cross culturally. European immigrants to the United States at the turn of the twentieth century permanently settled in as foreigners who really did not belong in the American mainstream. Their language and customs and attitudes marked them apart. Their children, a second generation, were accused by their "American" classmates of being foreigners, while at home their parents accused them of acting just like those "stupid Americans." The children of these children, the third generation, are fully enculturated and assimilated as "true" Americans, and more than that, they are very proud of their first-generation immigrant grandparents. They stay attached to their foods and often to their language and music as well.

The same process can be verified among the African American third generation, who are removed from slavery and are very interested in and proud of their grandparents' generation. Similarly, in the Philippines third-generation Samareños, whose grandparents emigrated from Samar to Tagalog-speaking Manila, want to know about the language and customs of Samar and the stories of their grandparents. Various third-generation African colonized persons are very interested in their first-generation ancestors, who "broke the bonds" of colonials. And third-generation Palestinians want to know the story of their grandparents prior to the Zionist criminal takeover of their lands and what those grandparents had to endure under Zionist Jewish supremacy; they are proud of their grandparents' stand in the face of continued Zionist atrocities and attempted genocide.

As far as ancient Israel is concerned, such significant and irreversible changes rooted in some appreciable social alterations include events such as:

- prior to the Persian period (about 500 BC), radical geo-graphical change and displacement, with little hope of return, for example, due to expulsion or forced one-way emigration or immigration during the formation of the so-called Diaspora;

- during the Persian period, with the formation of the Persian colony of Yahud south of Samaria and the adoption of Persian customs by the various peoples who worshiped the god Yah, third-generation Yahud people (later called Judeans), with their temple in Jerusalem, were proud of their Persian origins, as indicated by the adoption of many Persian customs (esoteric language of sacred writing, eternal flame in temple, etc.), as well as by the formation of a Parsee political-religious group (called Pharisees in the New Testament);

- during the Roman destruction of Israel's central temple (the center of political religion), the emergence of a new social structure or new social situation, for example, from prevailing political religion to newly exclusive fictive kinship religion.

In each of the foregoing cases, the first generation is disoriented by its experience of major modification of its social situation, making return to the old situation impossible. The second generation, emerging after the significant and irreversible social change, finds itself in tension with the new situation. The parent generation accuses it of departing from old ways, while the local population among which the second generation now finds itself accuses it of not adequately fitting in.

The second generation is an in-between generation. Predictably, the second generation either does not care to remember many dimensions of first-generation experiences or even wishes to ignore many aspects of the experiences that their elders considered so focal. The third generation, by contrast, shows interest in and wishes to remember and retrieve as much of that first-generation experience as it can. (Among Judeans, the work of third-generation scribes, called Tannaim, collected in the Mishnah, is indicative of this phase.) Third-generation people are always proud of their first-generation ancestors, founders, or originating groups. Thus focus of interest revealed in early Jesus-group documents serves as a, if not *the*, key to generational indications.

For example, second-generation Paul and his coworkers reveal little interest in the story of Jesus. From the Pauline writings, one might conclude that they were not interested in the story of Jesus at all. Paul's gospel of God is about what the God of Israel did for Israelites by raising Jesus from the dead. On the other hand, the Gospel stories of Matthew and Mark and John are third-generation products, marked by typical third-generation interests in their first-generation roots. Similarly, Luke's writings (as well as the letters to Timothy and Titus) are third-generation writings in the Pauline tradition, that is, the third generation after Paul and Timothy and the people mentioned in the authentic Pauline letters. Relative to Jesus, Luke's retelling of that story is the way a fourth-generation Jesus-group member thought it fit in to make sense of the second generation (Paul and friends), in which the writer was really interested.

And so we have two three-generation sequences to consider when assessing the New Testament documents. One of these sequences traces the line from Jesus to the generation of the Gospels of Matthew, Mark, and John; another traces the line from Paul and Timothy to the generation of Luke and the letters of 1–2 Timothy and Titus.

Defining Generation

The category of generation here refers to a group of living persons constituting a single step in the line of descent from an ancestor (either person or event). While the term has a temporal, chronological dimension, its main feature is sequential, a single step in a line of descent. The category can be applied to generations of those affiliated with Jesus. The first generation included

Jesus, his core-group members, their family members, along with friends and followers who belonged to their social network. They constituted Jesus' generation, and their contemporaries presumably included those addressed by Jesus in the Synoptic tradition as "this generation." [See in the triple tradition: "The Pharisees came and began to argue with him, seeking from him a sign from heaven, to test him. And he sighed deeply in his spirit, and said, 'Why does this generation seek a sign? Truly, I say to you, no sign shall be given to this generation'" (Mark 8:11-12//Matt 12:38-39 [16:1-4]//Luke 11:29); "And he [Jesus] answered them, 'O faithless generation, how long am I to be with you? How long am I to bear with you?'" (Mark 9:19//Matt 17:17//Luke 9:41); "Truly, I say to you, this generation will not pass away before all these things take place" (Mark 13:30//Matt 24:34//Luke 21:34); and in Q: "To what then shall I compare the men of this generation, and what are they like?" (Luke 7:31// Matt 11:16); ". . . the blood of all the prophets, shed from the foundation of the world, may be required of this generation, from the blood of Abel to the blood of Zechariah, who perished between the altar and the sanctuary. Yes, I tell you, it shall be required of this generation" (Luke 11:50-51//Matt 23:36).]

Paul and his collaborators (Timothy, Silvanus, Sosthenes, and others), with their contemporaries, in turn, marked a second step in the line of descent of this fictive kin group, a second generation. This generation consisted of Israelite Judeans and Israelite Greeks (i.e., Judeans and Hellenists, as in Gal 3:28; for the meaning of these terms, see chapter 5). Second-generation Judeans surely had information about Jesus' words (for example, the tradition common to Matthew and Luke called Q, sayings now found in the so-called Gospel of Thomas, perhaps a collection of Jesus' parables) and deeds (for example, a collection of anecdotes about Jesus' wondrous deeds). This information was largely in the form of lists, either to be cherished as keepsake from the first generation, still largely in control of Judean and Galilean Jesus groups, or ignored as irrelevant in the light of second-generation reinterpretations triggered by Jesus-group experience outside Judea and Galilee. As is usual, generations overlap, with members of the first step in the line of descent still alive, while the members of the second step emerge in the social arena. The disputes of Paul and his coworkers with first-generation Jesus-group leadership (as in Galatians, with Peter, James, and John) is typical of the interplay between first and second generations.

The writers of the Gospels according to Mark, Matthew, and John (in his distinctive way) belong to a third generation of Jesus-group members, a third step in the line of descent beginning with Jesus. It is the concern of these third-generation tradents to describe the "full" story of what Jesus said and did, as is typical of third-generation interests. Direct reference to such narratives as third-generation productions is offered by the fourth-generation writer of Luke-Acts, who mentions the "many [who] have undertaken to compile a narrative of the things which have been accomplished among us" (Luke 1:1). For the writer of Luke-Acts, these previous narratives stand at a third generation in a line of succession from Jesus. Luke-Acts itself belongs to a fourth generation of succession, since it utilizes and incorporates these many compiled narratives and recalls another, new first generation, that of Paul and his companions.

Other sources besides Luke-Acts witness to interest in generational step sequences. Consider Papias, bishop of Hierapolis, ca. 130), quoted by Eusebius of Caesarea (himself interested in such sequences):

> Five books of Papias are extant, bearing the title Expositions of the Oracles of the Lord. Irenaeus relates that this is his only work, and says, "Papias, the hearer of John and companion of Polycarp, a man of an earlier generation, testifies to these things in his fourth book. His work is in five volumes." Such is the evidence of Irenaeus. Now Papias himself in the introduction to his writings makes no claim to be a hearer and eyewitness of the holy Apostles, but to have received the contents of the faith from those that were known to them. He tells us this in his own words: "I shall not hesitate to set down for you, along with my interpretations, all things which I learned from the elders with care

and recorded with care, being well assured of their truth.
For, unlike most men, I took pleasure not in those that had
much to say but in those that teach the truth, not in those
who record strange precepts, but in those who relate such
precepts as were given to the faith from the Lord and are
derived from the truth itself. Besides, if ever any man came
who had been a follower of the elders, I would inquire
about the sayings of the elders; what Andrew said, or Peter,
or Philip, or Thomas, or James, or John, or Matthew, or any
other of the Lord's disciples; and what Aristion says, and
John the Elder, who are disciples of the Lord. For I did not
consider that I got so much profit from the contents of
books as from the utterances of a living and abiding voice.
(Eusebius, *Expositions of the Oracles of the Lord*, Historia
Ecclesiastica III.39)[4]

Papias thus gets his information from the followers of the elders.
He is third generation; the followers, second generation; and the
elders themselves, first generation.

The First Generation and the Jesus Story

Data about the first Jesus generation have been compiled by
the mass of scholars engaged in the quest for the "historical
Jesus." The historical Jesus is the Jesus experienced by first-
generation Jesus-group members. The first Jesus generation
consisted of the faction members gathered by Jesus along with
the subsequent coalition that awaited his return as Israel's
Messiah with power.

The term "faction" means a group of people gathered by some
central person for a given time to assist the faction founder in
his project. Jesus called a core group of persons to assist him in
the project of informing fellow Israelites about the forthcoming
Israelite theocracy. This new political-religious system was to
be established soon in Jerusalem and vicinity. The term "coalition" refers to any grouping of people who gather for a certain
purpose for a given time. In the story of Jesus, the people who

believed his prophetic proclamation and awaited the emergence of the kingdom of God in his generation formed this coalition.

For his generation, Jesus was God's holy man and prophet, what a Hellenist would call "a son of God." The original Galilean faction engaged in assisting Jesus in proclaiming a forthcoming Israelite theocracy and in preparing Israelites for the event through healing and exorcism. The theocracy would be ushered in by a celestial entity to whom Jesus referred as "the Son of man": "For whoever is ashamed of me and of my words in this adulterous and sinful generation, of him will the Son of man also be ashamed when he comes in the glory of his Father with his holy angels" (Mark 8:38//Matt 16:27; Luke 9:26). In his final, prescient discourse to his core group, Jesus mentions that this personage was expected to appear at the forthcoming destruction of the Jerusalem temple: "And then they will see the Son of man coming in clouds with great power and glory. And then he will send out the angels and gather his elect from the four winds, from the ends of the earth to the ends of heaven" (Mark 13:26-27//Matt 24:30-31//Luke 21:27). The reason for this is that this Son of man, who was with God from before the foundation of the world (Rev 12:5), was God's agent in wreaking satisfaction from Jerusalemites for Israel's dishonoring God (Rev 14:17-20).[5]

Any Israelite theocracy would be centered in Jerusalem and its temple. Jerusalem was Israel's sacred center, the place where God and God's people interacted in the sacred precincts of the temple. Any Israelites who wished to participate in the forthcoming theocracy would have to be acceptable for temple worship. According to Israel's traditions, the sick had to be healed and "cleansed" to fulfill requirements for temple worship (Lev 21:17-23, priestly rules applied to all Israelites by Pharisee scribes). Opponents of the forthcoming theocracy, "an adulterous generation," would not be allowed to stand before God in the temple: "No bastard shall enter the assembly of the LORD; even to the tenth generation none of his descendants shall enter the assembly of the LORD" (Deut 23:2; note Jesus' invective in Matt 12:39 and 16:4 against "an evil and adulterous generation"). A forthcoming theocracy meant Israelites had to get their affairs in order (repentance) and aligned with the will of the God of Israel.

After the political calamity of Jesus' crucifixion, the first Jesus generation found its hopes buoyed by the appearances of Jesus, whom they claimed to have experienced in their midst. To this they witnessed. As a fourth generation remembered, "God raised him on the third day and made him manifest, not to all the people but to us who were chosen by God as witnesses, who ate and drank with him after he was raised from the dead" (Acts 10:40-41). This statement from the Acts of the Apostles intimates that Jesus' faction interpreted Jesus' appearance as God's raising Jesus from the dead. This perspective is underscored by Paul, who notes that "five hundred" of the first generation "brothers" also saw the raised Jesus (1 Cor 15:6). This act of the God of Israel confirmed the suspicion of many in Jesus' entourage that Jesus was Israel's Messiah, who would accompany the forthcoming inauguration of a new Israelite theocracy.

From a generational perspective, the most significant, irreversible social change for Jesus groups was Jesus' death and subsequent appearance. The social outcome was the radical institutional transformation of the first generation from a political-religious faction in Israel to an Israelite political-religious party. A faction dissolves after the task specified by the central person is fulfilled. A party is a stable and enduring group. The book of Acts describes this institutional transformation. First-generation Jesus-group interest was in an immediately forthcoming theocracy (kingdom of God/heaven) ushered in by a celestial Son of man. With the resurrection of Jesus, this interest was altered by the notion that Jesus was indeed Israel's Messiah, who himself would usher in the theocracy.

The first Jesus generation developed into a new Jesus-group coalition that took its rightful place in Judea as an Israelite political-religious party. This political-religious party believed that when Jesus the Messiah arrived with power, Israel's expected political-religious theocracy would materialize. This Jesus-group party advocated broader Israelite awareness of the forthcoming theocracy, with Jesus as Israel's Messiah and God's agent. The group was as temple-focused as Jesus was (Acts 2:46 and passim; Paul, too, is concerned with the temple tax collection for the poor in Jerusalem: Rom 15:26; Gal 2:10), presumably expecting Israel's Messiah to appear soon in the temple precinct, marking the onset of a new political-religious regime in Israel.

In sum, this first generation held the belief that God would establish a theocracy in Israel soon, ushered in by Jesus, Israel's Messiah. In Luke's fourth-generation story, note that the burden of Jesus' discussions with his inner circle in the forty days after his death was in fact the kingdom of God (Acts 1:3), after which they ask him: "Lord, will you at this time restore the kingdom to Israel?" (Acts 1:6). The answer is a fourth-generation answer: "It is not for you to know times or seasons which the Father has fixed by his own authority" (Acts 1:7). Concern for the forthcoming theocracy was the pervasive first-generation concern if only because this is what Jesus himself proclaimed and what he had charged his assisting disciples to proclaim. This concern continues through the second generation.

The Second Generation and What God Did to Jesus

The failure of the Israelite theocracy to quickly materialize created a sense of concern for the second generation. Given their collectivistic, ethnocentric outlook, those who shared belief in the coming of Israel's theocracy and of Messiah Jesus felt impelled to take up the task of informing all Israelites of the event soon to transpire. While first-generation personages such as Peter, James, John, and their contemporaries eventually took up this task of proclaiming theocracy to Israelites in their social (Judean) and geographical vicinity, a second-generation Jesus-group member, Paul, and a number of his colleagues and clients took the proclamation to distant Israelite communities in cities with non-Israelite majorities.[6]

Paul was a second-generation Jesus-group member. In the recollections of the writer of the Acts of the Apostles, we find him as a youth collecting the garments of those who stoned one Stephen (Acts 7:58). Whether factual or not, this notice indicates that in the perspective of the writer of the book of Acts, Paul belonged to the second generation. In the letter to the Galatians, Paul himself attests that previously "he persecuted the church of God violently" (Gal 1:13). This indicates that he knew very well what Jesus-group members believed and how they behaved. We know that Paul later lived for a time with Jesus-group members in Arabia and Damascus (Gal 1:17-18). His problems with Cephas (Peter's name in Aramaic, which Paul always uses: Gal 2:11-14) attest to expected intergenerational conflict, ultimately rooted in conflicting institutional structures—one, a political religion (the Jerusalem Jesus-group focused on the temple); the other, a domestic religion (various Jesus groups focused on households). What was the predictable nature of this conflict?

The second generation had little interest in retaining focused attention on what was of significance to the first, while the first generation found objectionable much of what the second did.

What was it about the first generation that the second generation wished to forget? Several things come to mind.

- That the first generation sought to revitalize Israel and to retain the past rather than relinquish it. The second generation, on the other hand, came to realize that with Jesus something new and better had begun to emerge—not a revitalized old covenant, but a new and better covenant with the God of Israel (note the scope of the "mission charge": Mark 3:13-19a; 6:7 and parallels). First-generation concerns about Judean customs (circumcision, kosher rules, calendar), part and parcel of Israel's political religion in Judea, were of little use and no concern to second-generation Jesus-group members living as minorities in majority non-Israelite cities. Second-generation Paul and his coworkers were little interested in Judean customs; they proclaimed their gospel among Diaspora Israelites and showed little concern for non-Israelites (see Rom 11:13-32 about the unnatural non-Israelite presence in Jesus groups in Rome).

- That the teachings of Jesus remembered by the first generation were inadequate and insufficient for the new covenant revealed in Jesus' being raised by the God of Israel. Second-generation Paul and his coworkers, for example, do not cite Jesus' words and deeds as norms; norms for their Jesus-group members derive from the spirit (see 1 Cor 12).

- The first generation believed that Jesus was a holy man and a prophet, a new Elijah and new Moses, even Israel's Messiah, but not someone of a quality entirely different from other Israelites. The second generation, held by the significance of Jesus' being raised from the dead by the God of Israel, viewed Jesus as more than Israel's Messiah; the resurrected Jesus was seated at God's right hand. He was cosmic Lord.

- That the first generation wished to have privileged participation in Israel's forthcoming theocracy rather than show concern for all Israel, including Israelite colonials (see the traditions about precedence in Mark 9:34//Matt 18:1//Luke 9:46; Mark 10:37//Matt 20:21); the second generation developed interest in all Israelites, including émigré families and colonials.

Furthermore, the larger Israelite society in which the two generations of Jesus-group members lived likewise found the second, upcoming generation highly objectionable. What was it about the second generation that made it objectionable, the object of criticism, to the first generation and the object of rejection by its contemporary Israelites?

Criticism by the first generation (indicating that second-generation members were not behaving as true Israelite followers of Jesus, hence deviant) included:

- its lack of interest in what exactly Jesus said and did; these were of secondary or no concern. Aside from the household ceremony of the Lord's Supper, the words and deeds of Jesus are not cited in second-generation writings.

- their focus shifted to what the God of Israel did to Jesus, not simply to Jesus' proclamation of an Israelite theocracy. While they awaited the forthcoming kingdom of God, their new emphasis was on God's activity, on what God did to Jesus and the present role of the resurrected Jesus. For the second generation, the Jesus group, in its domestic religion, is God's temple, where the spirit of the resurrected Jesus is found (1 Cor 3 and 6).[7]

- in the light of what God did to Jesus, the second generation displaced the directive role of Israel's Torah in favor of the presence of the Spirit of Jesus (see Paul's description of charisms from the spirit: 1 Cor 12).

All these features can be found in the Pauline letters.

On the other hand, criticism by Israelite contemporaries of second-generation Jesus-group members (indicating they are not truly Israelite, hence apostates) includes the objections that they proclaimed:

- a forthcoming theocracy for Israel, thus implying a rejection of existing arrangements: priesthood, parties, temple styles (for example, Paul and coworkers considered Jesus groups as God's temple: 1 Cor 3:17; 6:19; 2 Cor 6:16).

- Jesus as Israel's Messiah soon to come, thus offering pretext for Romans to squeeze Israel's polity, its political religion (clearly recalled in John 11:48).

- their attitude toward the binding nature of traditional Pharisaic Torah interpretation. Second-generation Jesus-group members took up behaviors characteristic of those of Israelites in the Diaspora rather than those of scribal Pharisees in Judea (for example, unconcern for circumcision in 1 Cor 7:19).

In face of the first Jesus generation, the second generation emphasized the presence of the Spirit of Jesus now, with the forthcoming presence of Jesus soon. This is second-generation *soonology* or *proximatology* (there is no eschatology, the so-called end times expectations).[8] With focus on the present and on what Jesus does now, there was little or no place for the Jesus of the past, the Jesus whose words and deeds were witnessed by the first generation.

Against their contemporary fellow Israelites, the second generation emphasized the role of Jesus as Israel's Messiah and cosmic Lord, with hope in a forthcoming Israelite theocracy. Since this notion derived from God's raising Jesus from the dead, as witnessed by the first generation and as experienced in Jesus' spirit events, obviously those who believed in Christ Jesus were true Israel, true Judeans. Their norms were grounded in their present experiences of Jesus through the spirit, hence in Israel's Torah traditions as interpreted through their present experiences of Jesus, not as interpreted through Israel's scribes accommodating and supporting the status quo.

What the First Generation Remembered and the Second Ignored

First generations have not only their history but also their historical recollections.[9] The collection of descriptions of significant events and sayings of Jesus would begin almost as early as the re-formed political-religious party itself (for example, Luke recalls this in the kerygma or proclamation described in Acts 3–9). The various lists of Jesus' sayings (Q; Gospel of Thomas), the songs about what God had done through Jesus (such as the psalms known as the *Benedictus* and *Magnificat* in Luke 1:46-55; 68-79), about his Davidic roots (Rom 1:3-4), remembrances of what he did (Passover Haggada questions: Mark 12:13-37)—all such lists of sayings or anecdotes, hymns, and admonitions constituted history, collective remembrances. Like memories in general, they were rather uncritical. There was much to be recounted, of course. The aging first-generation participants in the Jesus movement got together to tell one another of the glorious deeds that they had seen and sometimes performed (note the meetings mentioned in Acts 2:46). They listened to the stories of Jesus whom they continued to experience in altered states of consciousness.[10] When the last of the first-generation group members had joined their ancestors, the first-generation groups automatically dissolved, leaving to their heirs as the first chapter of Jesus-group historiography a conglomerate mass of information in prepared or extemporaneous lists.

Second-generation Jesus-group members were totally taken by what the God of Israel had done to Jesus, not with what Jesus himself said and did. In that activity, the God of Israel revealed himself now as "he who raised Christ Jesus from the dead" (Rom 8:11). More than that, the God of Israel exalted Jesus and made him Lord and Christ (Phil 2:9-11; Acts 2:33; 5:31). Developing an incipient theory of who Jesus might really be (called "Christology") was a second-generation activity, revealing interest in Jesus' origins paralleling developing insight into the ramifications of what God did to Jesus and what significance this had for Jesus' followers. A hymn like that of Phil 2:6-11 or the cosmic visions of Revelation point to such interest.

While various, largely Judean second-generation persons obviously preserved the first-generation lists of what Jesus said and did, the second-generation documents that we have showed little interest in what Jesus himself said and did. Jesus was now located with the God of Israel, above the celestial vault of the sky, over Jerusalem. As later documents recall, there he was taken by God (fourth generation, Acts 1:9), was seen by Stephen (fourth generation, Acts 7:56), and was observed as the cosmic Lamb of God by the seer of Revelation in his throne vision (third generation, Rev 4–5).

With new focus on what God had done to Jesus, the political-religious activity of Jesus among Galileans, Pereans, and Judeans was considered inadequate and uninteresting, a thing of the past, of a previous generation. Second-generation Jesus groups rejected Israelite political religion along with Jesus "descended from David according to the flesh" (Rom 1:3). By doing so, they generally, though not universally, distanced themselves both from the Jesus who came "in the likeness of sinful flesh" (Rom 8:3) and from Israelite political religion. They developed a Jesus-group domestic religion, a fictive household of brothers and sisters in Christ focused on the deeds of the God of Israel in their present experience of the spirit, as they awaited the establishment of God's kingdom in Jerusalem.

Second-generation Jesus-group members came to embrace the divinely inaugurated Jesus innovation not merely as people seeking something new and better, but as members of the house of Israel. Jesus was Christ and Lord for all Israel, not just Judeans, Galileans and Pereans. For the most part they constituted both an ethnic group (the label "Messiah/Christ" is ethnic) as well as a fictive kin group with an embedded fictive domestic religion (the "in" part of the phrase "in Christ"). Thus "in Christ" designated both without distinction. Both in Palestine and in the émigré Greco-Roman world, Jesus-group communities were ethnically Israelite, yet with a distinctive domestic religion. So it was understood by all except the few non-Israelites who later joined Jesus groups and sought to replace its Israelite ethnic character by something more catholic (perhaps first indicated by the post-Pauline third-generation letter to the Ephesians).

The mental mobility characteristic of Israelite residents living as minorities in non-Israelite cities both facilitated this process and in turn was spurred by it. As Paul and his coworkers conveyed their second-generation proclamation of the gospel of God, this gospel was accepted by innovators and first adopters who prospered economically and culturally, and were largely assimilated into Greco-Roman urban societies. This assimilation of Jesus-group Israelite "Greeks" quickened the movement of these Jesus groups away from the practices of the Israelite homeland.

Israelite identity remained firm from the first to the second generation. Yet second-generation Jesus groups were found both in Palestine and its vicinity as well as in more distant non-Israelite cities. The former continued to adhere to Israelite political religion as a Jesus-group political-religious party. Undoubtedly the Peter/John/James group(s) and their successors and friends in Judea and Galilee, as well as cities with a large Israelite population, such as Alexandria and Antioch, remained an Israelite political party until the destruction of Jerusalem in AD 70. From their ranks came those whom Paul and Timothy called "Judaizers," located in Palestine and elsewhere "among the circumcised." They made Judean customs a requirement for membership in Israelite Jesus groups. However, it seems that most of those Judean customs were abandoned among Hellenized Israelites living among non-Israelite majorities, the population among whom Paul proclaimed his gospel of God and from which Timothy came.[11] It was among those groups that the fictive domestic religious expressions of Jesus-group ideology developed.

Third Generation

As the writings of second-generation Jesus-group members demonstrate, the sons were not interested in the stories of the fathers. As a broad generalization, it may be said that the second generation was not interested in, and did not write, any narrative history. That is another aspect of their rather unaware policy of forgetting.[12] However, after the second generation came a third. With this third generation there usually appeared a new force and a new opportunity. In the case of Jesus-group development, this third generation performed the task of salvaging first-generation memories and undoubtedly accomplished more than either the first or the second could ever have achieved. The Gospel stories, now put in the written forms of Mark, Matthew, and John (and "many" others noted by Luke 1:1-4), are just one feature of their achievements.

With the Roman destruction of Jerusalem and its institutional arrangements, Pharisaic scribes organized into a form best described as first-generation Ben Zakkaist scribalism (named after Johannan ben Zakkai, a legendary Pharisaic leader at the time of Jerusalem's destruction). Post-destruction Pharisee groups resided in the same Israelite quarters as third-generation Jesus groups. In their own way, these Pharisee groups pushed third-generation Jesus-group members to maturity, making affiliations based upon some remote Jesus-group ancestors in Jerusalem ever less meaningful. The old customary belonging markers, too much like those of Ben Zakkaists, were allowed to shrivel and disappear. The Judean Jesus groups themselves, in their older political-religious forms at least, became less and less intelligible and relevant to present third-generation Jesus-group reality.

The emergence of the third-generation Jesus groups was accompanied by the approaching dissolution of Israelite political religion, marked by the destruction of Jerusalem. The first generation of Jesus groups, like Jesus himself, had been devoted to that political religion, while the second generation outside of Palestine and perhaps in Galilee distanced itself from it. True to Hansen's schema, the third generation, secure in its associational structure and values, was willing and eager to "remember" what the second generation had been so eager to "forget."

Along with the written Gospels, another third-generation phenomenon was intermarriage within the same domestic religious group regardless of status. Jesus-group members would give their children in marriage within their group, a reapplication and replication of Mediterranean endogamy. Intermarriage within the Jesus-group community was rapid and unhampered, since Jesus groups formed a new, third category, neither Judean barbarians nor Greek civilized persons, but Messianists, that is, "Christians" (on this third type, see *Letter to Diognetus*, prologue; Aristides, *Apologia* 2; Clement of Alexandria, *Stromata* VI 41.6-7; on third-generation marriage, see also Ignatius of Antioch, *Letter to Polycarp* 5).

In the same way, the earlier tendencies toward local assimilation were carried further with the third generation. The evolving lifestyle of the group fell imperceptibly into the mold of *polis* (city) culture, although it retained distinctive features derived from the past. This trend was one characteristic of all groups undergoing irreversible social change as they became resocialized and developed new goals and standards. The difference between Israelites and non-Israelites in the same region was one of degree rather than of kind (a process begun by various generations of Israelite émigrés).

In utilizing the story of Jesus as ideology supporting its articulation of social identity, Jesus-group fictive kin-group associations themselves underwent significant change. Prior to the fall of Jerusalem, Israelites belonged to various political associations: first-generation Jesus groups, Pharisees, Herodians, Essenes, later Zealots, and the like. These groups were based less on theological than social distinctions and political goals. After the fall of the City in AD 70, all of the many parties that comprised the Israelite political-religious social scene were still there, but in transformed shape. They took on the new and unique social structure developed outside Palestine previously by some Israelite émigrés: the fictive kin group cum ethnically based domestic religion. Jesus groups had adopted this sort of social structure a generation earlier with their second-generation groups situated among "the Foreskins," as Paul called non-Israelites (Gal 2:7).

With the demise of Jerusalem, other such groups took on this structure, notably Jesus groups among "the Circumcision," the Ben Zakkaists, Zealots, and the Sadducees (later Karaites). Some of these soon reconstituted in Jerusalem as political-religious parties; others survived as fictive kin groups. But with the final destruction of Jerusalem and expulsion of Judeans in AD 135, all Israelite parties followed the lead taken by Jesus-movement groups two generations earlier.

In sum, what the third generation of Jesus groups sought to remember was the first generation and its experience of Jesus. This first generation was considered to be witness to the experience of Jesus, the root-ancestor generation. The remembering of the third generation took the form of the story of Jesus. As third-generation remembrance, Jesus stories were appropriated and elaborated, told with a view to relevance in new situations, recontextualized after a fashion. Each version had a different general purpose that satisfied third-generation requirements to learn the story of its origins and to find meaning in its details.

Fourth-Generation Luke-Acts and
Another Third-Generation Line of Descent

Along with the story of Jesus, there is also another "biography" in the New Testament, that of Paul (said to be of Tarsus by the writer of Luke-Acts, who crafted this biography; see Acts 9:11; 21:39; 22:3). According to the book of Acts, the story of Paul is about that well-known second-generation "Judean" Jesus-group member, Saul (alias Paul), who took the gospel of God to Israelites living in predominantly non-Israelite Greco-Roman *poleis* (Mediterranean cities). These "diaspora" Israelite adopters of Paul's gospel of God were almost exclusively Hellenized Israelites, "Greeks."

Among those Greeks, Paul recruited one Timothy, residing in the town of Lystra. Timothy's father was a Greek, while his mother was a Judean (Acts 16:1-3). As Paul attests, the house of Israel in this period consisted of "Judeans and Greeks," that is barbarians and civilized Israelite persons, who might become one in Christ.

Those who accepted Paul's proclamation and embraced his practice formed a first-generation line of descent from Saul/Paul. Of course, this included Timothy, his parents, and Paul's other coworkers. Their focus was on the hope of the proximate advent of an Israelite theocracy. When that theocracy failed to appear, the generation after Paul and Timothy, that is, the second-generation Pauline Jesus groups, developed alternatives to awaiting the theocracy. A second generation within the Pauline line included the people addressed in the second letter to the Thessalonians. As this writing shows, this generation demonstrated no concern for the life of Paul and none for the life of Jesus. And its rules for social organization indicate a sense of permanence, unrelated to what Paul said and did among them, since a number believed that the "Day of the Lord," the inauguration of the kingdom, had already come. This second Pauline generation was contemporary with the third generation of Jesus groups that produced the Gospels.

The subsequent third Pauline generation, by contrast, wanted to know and recall what Paul and his coworkers were like, what they did, how knowledge of Paul's version of the gospel of God had come down to it. Such third-generation interest in the life of Paul is to be found in Luke-Acts, as well as in references in the letters to Timothy, Titus, Colossians, and Ephesians. These latter are ostensibly third Pauline-generation writings, and fourth Jesus-group generation writings.

Consider Luke's articulation of the four generations that developed from the original experience of Jesus (Luke 1:1-4). The writer belonged to a fourth generation, within which a number of narratives (*diegeseis*, that is, third-generation Jesus-group stories) recounting what Jesus said and did have emerged. These narratives were based, Luke says, on what was handed down (presumably, by a second generation), tracing back to the "eye-witnesses and ministers of the word" (first generation). "Handing down" (*paradidonai*) is different from, and secondary to, direct attestation. Handing down requires intermediaries, in this case a second generation, with a third generation constituting the storytellers.

> Inasmuch as many [third generation] have undertaken to compile a narrative of the things which have been accomplished among us, just as they were delivered to us [second generation] by those who from the beginning were eyewitnesses and ministers of the word [first generation], it seemed good to me [fourth generation] also, having followed all things closely for some time past, to write an orderly account for you, most excellent Theophilus, that you [fourth generation] may know the truth concerning the things of which you have been informed. (Luke 1:1-4)

Luke relates his "orderly account" to other "narratives" of the previous Jesus-group generation and the traditions they used. Those traditions consisted of lists, collections of sayings and anecdotes of deeds put together in some unconnected fashion.

While Luke's story of Jesus is much like those other third Jesus-group generation writings called Matthew and Mark, what is significant is his second volume. In that volume (called the Acts of the Apostles), Luke further describes first-generation Jesus-group activity in Judea and Samaria, but, most distinctively, he narrates the story of Paul and Paul's second-generation coworkers. His telling the story of Paul identifies him as a member in the third generation in line of descent from Paul, living in a city with an Israelite Hellenistic Jesus-group founded by Paul. As has been pointed out by Talbert long ago,[13] Luke's story of Paul and his immediate predecessors runs as a diptych or parallel to the story of Jesus. Tradition has it that "Luke" was from Ephesus; in his Acts narrative, the Ephesians were the last Asian Jesus group that Paul visited (at Miletus) before he left for Jerusalem, where he was arrested (see Acts 20:17-38).

It seems rather easy to describe the post-Pauline concerns of the second- and third-generational line of descent finally expressed in Luke's story of Paul in the Acts of the Apostles. Following Hansen, one can see that the New Testament documents attest to "the almost universal phenomenon that what the son wishes to forget the grandson wishes to remember." In the case of Paul, his "sons," such as the writer(s) of 2 Thessalonians, tell of those who selectively chose to forget the Pauline letters. What Paul actually said and did was irrelevant to their second Pauline-generation interests and social situation, despite their attributing those interests to Paul, Silvanus, and Timothy. Their interest, however, was not in what Paul said and did, but in the relevance of Paul's gospel in their new social circumstances. By contrast, for the third Pauline generation, it was precisely the details of the story of Paul, his call by the God of Israel, and his activity among Israelites resident in cities with non-Israelite majorities that were important for the third-generation "grandson" Luke (as well as the documents called Timothy and Titus).

In sum, in accord with the principle of third-generation interest, third-generation Jesus groups in the Judean culture area showed interest in Jesus' story, in his career and the original context of his kingdom proclamation. This interest, however, did not derive from any actual hope for a forthcoming kingdom or from vital symbolic value attributed to theocracy, but from third-generation interest in the past. This is a form of ancestor reverence. The first Jesus generation developed its remembrances of Jesus in lists of anecdotes and sayings, collected or free-floating, all of which was of little vital interest to the second generation. It likewise cherished its scriptural understanding of Jesus' death and resurrection and devised a ritual of group initiation and a ceremony of group belonging focused on remembrance of Jesus' final meal.

The second generation was taken by what God had done to Jesus, specifically his raising Jesus from the dead. Their question about where Jesus was now entailed what it meant for the God of Israel to be "he who raised Jesus from the dead" and also interest in Jesus' present role with a view to the forthcoming kingdom of God. It also attended to what the first generation had witnessed and handed down in brief lists of scriptural passages strung together as important ingredients of a story of Jesus' crucifixion, death, and being raised by God (see 1 Cor 15:3-7). And it continued first-generation group-initiation practices (baptism) and continued to practice, in memory of Jesus, what the first generation said that Jesus was said to have requested (see 1 Cor 11:23-26). Mark and Matthew (and perhaps John) constructed narratives demonstrating third-generation interests. Luke is different, as we learn from his prologue and second volume, the Acts of the Apostles. The "life" of Paul in Acts indicates that the writer was a third-generation writer in the Pauline line, hence a fourth-generation Jesus-group member.

Conclusion

The contents of the New Testament Gospels and the Acts of the Apostles have the same degree of accuracy as high-context third-generation documents in general. The third-generation narratives are reappropriations of events and stories that are now made applicable to the situations of third-generation audiences. The third Jesus generation was interested in telling a story based on first-generation information as well as in establishing its fictive kinship norms of social identity and social interaction. For the third generation, the coming kingdom proclaimed by Jesus will be Israel's final, definitive kingdom. It will last forever. But "final," "definitive," and "forever" have to be interpreted in terms of ancient Mediterranean perceptions of duration and the future, categories that are imaginary.[14] The forthcoming is rather certain, the future is totally uncertain. Hopes for a final kingdom are simply hopes. That final kingdom is not unlike the rule of the house of David that would last "forever," that is, until it ceased with the last Davidic heir.

In this context, then, who was Timothy? Timothy was a second-generation Jesus-group member. We find him assisting Paul, obviously as a member of that first Pauline generation. From the Pauline letters, we know for sure that Timothy was a valued coworker of Paul's, a co-sender of a number of Pauline letters, and a dear friend of Paul throughout the course of his activities, from the time of Paul's first foundation at Thessalonika to the time of his planned trip to Spain with a stopover in Rome. The book of Acts notes that this final part of Paul's plan did not turn out the way Paul expected. Nevertheless, Timothy was with Paul for nearly the whole duration of Paul's activity, spanning the whole second Jesus generation. From the fourth Jesus-generation writings of Luke-Acts, we learn what that generation wished to remember of Timothy: that he met up initially with Paul at Lystra, where Timothy lived in good repute with his Israelite parents, a Judean mother and a Greek father; that Paul recruited him (in Barnabas's place, as we shall see); that he labored as Paul's co-worker throughout Paul's career. From those equally fourth Jesus-generation documents called the letters to Timothy, we get further information about how Timothy was remembered.

To determine what Timothy actually was doing, we shall now turn to a consideration of what Paul was up to and how Timothy fit into Paul's activities.

First generation	Second generation	Third generation	Fourth generation
Jesus and his disciples No writing	Paul, Silvanus Timothy, Sosthenes Pauline Authentic Letters	Mark, Matthew John, 2 Thess Revelation	Luke 1–2 Timothy, Titus Colossians Ephesians, Hebrews
Collection of words and deeds of Jesus	Collection of words of Paul/Timothy	Story of Jesus	Story of Paul and Timothy and Titus
Jesus groups	Judean Messiah Jesus Groups Greek Lord Jesus Groups	Judean Messiah Jesus Groups Greek Lord Jesus Groups	Greek Lord Jesus Groups
Focus: proclamation of Kingdom	group formation based on coming Kingdom	Jesus' celestial activity as we await the Kingdom	reformed group formation with Kingdom in abeyance

Judean Messiah-Jesus groups include first-generation Jesus followers, second-generation Jesus-group members, such as the "Judaizers," (Galatians, Colossians), and third-generation Jesus-group members focused on Jesus' celestial activity.

Second-generation Judean-Messiah Jesus groups were concerned with group-definition in terms of symbols about the Messiah Jesus (James goes here), while third-generation Judean-Messiah Jesus groups were concerned with the story of Jesus (Mark, Matthew, and John) and with what Jesus is doing now relative to Israel (Revelation).

Third-generation Jesus groups that constituted second-generation Pauline Greek Lord Jesus groups were much concerned with the activities of Jesus as Lord. The answer to what Jesus is doing now is provided by documents from this generation in the Pauline tradition.

Fourth-generation Jesus groups have little concern with Jesus as Messiah (at least as far as their documents are concerned). These documents are largely third-generation Pauline Greek Lord Jesus groups, concerned with the story of Paul (which mirrors the story of Jesus and is directed by the resurrected Jesus) and includes a restatement of Paul's directives to group leaders of this generation.

CHAPTER 3

Timothy as Assistant to Paul: What Was Paul Up To?

I n their collective memory of their ancestors in faith, Christians often leave Timothy out of focus, while the apostle Paul holds center stage. Yet it seems that one cannot really recount the story of Paul as evidenced from the letters of Paul (and others) without mentioning his trusted and devoted aide. Paul calls Timothy his trustworthy and beloved son in the Lord (1 Cor 4:17); one who deeply shares his outlook (Phil 5:20); a partner in his activity in the Lord (1 Cor 16:10); his coworker or collaborator (Rom 16:21); his brother and fellow minister of God (1 Thess 3:2); a slave of Jesus Christ (Phil 1:1), devoted to the cause of Christ (Phil 2:21).

Many first-century Israelites joined Jesus-movement groups because they heard Paul proclaim the gospel of God. No less than for others in the Pauline Jesus groups, the same holds for Timothy: "For though you have countless guides in Christ, you do not have many fathers. For I became your father in Christ Jesus through the gospel" (1 Cor 4:14-15). Paul had such confidence in Timothy that he could send him to deal with problems that arose in the Corinthian Jesus groups: "Therefore I sent to you Timothy, my beloved and faithful child in the Lord, to remind you of my ways in Christ, as I teach them everywhere in every church" (1 Cor 4:16-17).

We learn nothing from the Pauline letters about where Timothy came from or about when he heard the gospel of God for the first time. However, these letters likewise say nothing of where Paul was from. This information comes two generations later, in the work called the Acts of the Apostles. However, the fact that Timothy could remind the Corinthians about Paul's Gospel and its ramification points to Timothy's close association with Paul. It also underscores the fact that if Bible readers want to learn about what Timothy was doing, they need some idea of what Paul was up to. In this chapter we consider Paul's project and how Timothy fit into that project.

Paul's Project

Paul frequently insists that he has been "called by the will of God to be an apostle" (1 Cor 1:1; see also 1 Thess 2:6; 1 Cor 4:9; 9:1-2; 15:9; 2 Cor 1:1; 11:5; 12:11-12; Gal 1:1; Rom 1:1, 5; 11:13). "Apostle" is a Greek word, not translated but transliterated (transcribed from the Greek alphabet into the Roman alphabet). In Greek the word refers to someone commissioned by someone else for some mission or task. Apostles can be sent for various reasons. Cynic philosophers were described as messengers of the God Zeus sent with the commission of making people aware of how to live properly (Epictetus, *Discourses* 3.22.23). Paul believed that he was an apostle of the God of Israel because he was commissioned to proclaim "the gospel of God" (1 Thess 2:2, 8, 9; Rom 1:1).

This gospel of God was an innovation wrought by the God of Israel in raising Jesus of Nazareth from the dead, with a view to a forthcoming Israelite theocracy. Paul was to communicate this innovation to his fellow Israelites living amid non-Israelites. He was to be a change agent in the service of the agency of the God of Israel. An apostle of Paul's type was, in fact, a change agent. In the letter to the Galatians (1:11-24) Paul offers a somewhat lengthy description of how he was commissioned. It happened in an altered or alternate state-of-consciousness experience through which the God of Israel revealed Jesus Christ to him "in order that I might preach him among the Gentiles" (Gal 1:16).

Altered States-of-Consciousness Experience

At this point it might be useful to explain what such "altered states of consciousness" are, since they are mentioned throughout the New Testament documents.[1] Anthropologists studying cross-cultural psychology define altered states of consciousness as conditions in which sensations, perceptions, cognition, and emotions are altered. Such states are characterized by changes in sensing, perceiving, thinking, and feeling. When a person is in such a state, the experience modifies the relation of the individual to the self, body, and sense of identity, and the environment of time, space, or other people. In trances, visions, or any other altered state of consciousness a person encounters, indeed enters, another level or aspect of reality registered physiologically in the brain in the same way "normal" experiences are. Culturally "normal" or consensus reality is that aspect or dimension of reality of which a person is most commonly aware most of the time. Alternate reality describes that dimension of reality in which non-human personages such as spirits and/or the deity reside, and which human beings from culturally "normal" reality can sometimes visit in ecstatic trance by taking a journey (variously called "sky journey" or "soul–loss," and the like), and to which people go when they die. The experience of alternate reality is non-rational but not irrational, as claimed by those who have not experienced, and hence do not believe, any of these things. From the perspective of these non-believing persons, such experiences would be appropriately described as experiences of non-consensual reality.

During the centuries before and after Paul, countless persons reported a range of visions and appearances involving celestial entities. Their experiences have to be interpreted within the framework of their own culture's consensus reality rather than ours. There is no reason not to take seriously what these persons say of their experiences just because they differ from ours. Paul ascribes his call by the God of Israel to his change-agent task to an altered state-of-consciousness experience initiated by God (Gal 1:1, 12). His descriptions of Jesus-group experiences, which he ascribes to God's Spirit, are all instances of such altered-state events. He himself notes his sky journey, in which he experienced the ineffable, in "Paradise" (2 Cor 12:1-7). Paradise in Israelite lore, of course, was the name of the garden of delight created by God for the first human beings (Gen 2). However, by Paul's day this place of blessedness was transposed into the sky (see Luke 23:43), often referred to as the third or highest level of the sky, where the righteous dead dwelt, awaiting the resurrection of the dead. Paul himself frequently receives directives from the realm of God (Rom 16:26; Gal 2:2; 2 Cor 12:8; Gal 2:2). Of course, Paul ascribes the visions of the resurrected Jesus to such altered-state experiences (1 Cor 15:5-8).

Aside from dreams and angelic appearances, the Synoptics report five main incidents of such visions and/or appearances in the career of Jesus—two by Jesus: at his baptism (Mark 1:9-11//Matt 3:13-17//Luke 3:21-22) and at his being tested as holy man (Mark 1:12-13//Matt 4:1-11//Luke 4:1-13); and three by various disciples: their vision of Jesus walking on the Sea of Galilee (Mark 6:45-52//Matt 14:22-33//John 6:16-21); their vision of Jesus transformed (Mark 9:2-10//Matt 17:1-9//Luke 9:28-36); and finally the various resurrection appearances, including the final appearance of Jesus, in God's name, commissioning the apostles to proclaim the gospel of God.

In the book of Acts, there is a virtually endless series of episodes depicting people in altered state-of-consciousness experiences: 1:1-11 (the ascension of the risen Jesus); 2:1-4 (the descent of the Spirit); 2:5-13 (glossolalia); 6:1–8:3 (Stephen, 7:55-56); 8:4-40 (Philip); 9:1-9 (Paul); 9:10-19 (Ananias); 9:43–10:8 (Cornelius); 10:9-16 (Peter); 10:17-23 (interpretation of Peter's vision); 10:23-48 (the soldier's house in Caesarea: Cornelius repeats; Peter explains;

glossolalia; trance experience); 11:1-18 (Peter explains in Jerusalem); 12:5-19 (Peter escapes arrest); 12:13-17 (the maid's reaction); 13:1-3 (commission in Antioch); 13:4-12 (Paul and the curse); 14:1-20 (healing); 16:6-10 (altered state-of-consciousness experience of the Spirit); 18:1-17 (Paul encouraged by the Lord); 18:18–19:4 (glossolalia in Corinth); 20:23 (experience of the Spirit); 22:6-21 (Paul's vision); 23:10-11 (the Lord speaks to Paul); 26:9-18 (Paul's vision, again); 27:23-26 (angel tells Paul his destiny). The whole book of Revelation depends upon the altered state-of-consciousness experiences of the prophet John.[2] This may be difficult for us to believe because we have been enculturated to be selectively inattentive to such states of awareness except in dreams and under the influence of controlled substances. They are not part of our consensus reality.

As Paul amply indicates by his use of Israel's sacred writings and themes from Israel's dealings with God, his gospel of God is a gospel of the God of Israel destined for Israelites. As his letters intimate, his task was to proclaim his Gospel to Israelites living "among the Gentiles." His high-context statement thus means: "to proclaim God's resurrected Jesus to Israelites living among non-Israelites."

Commissioning by one with authority is sufficient to make a person an apostle. But Paul was not simply authorized by the God of Israel to make a proclamation, but a proclamation of something new in and for Israel, something hitherto unheard of. Consequently, if the gospel of God proclaimed by Paul had any distinctive quality, it was the fact that it was something new, something unheard of, perhaps even something inconceivable.

Paul took up the task of communicating this innovation to his fellow Israelites. What exactly did he do? There are few data in the high-context Pauline writings to fill out a picture of his activities. The book of the Acts of the Apostles, written two generations after Paul and Timothy, does provide a conceptual pattern of Paul's initial contacts with his fellow Israelites. To formulate a working pattern, I shall fill in the blanks, so to say, by using models from the social sciences that describe what the diffusion of an innovation entails. The models employed here are presented at a somewhat higher level of abstraction in order to cluster similarities. They have been cross-culturally verified with a range of data drawn from all over the world. This should support the idea that they are cross-temporally valid as well. The diffusion of an innovation follows a rather fixed social pattern of interaction.[3]

The Apostle as Change Agent

As a rule, a change agent is an authorized person who influences innovation decisions in a direction deemed desirable by a change agency. An apostle is a person sent by some commissioning agent for some purpose. A change agent is a type of apostle, one sent to promote and launch an innovation. Paul was a Jesus-group change agent. The change agent functions as a communication link between two or more entities—that of the receivers of the communication, the clients, and that of the change agency, the one(s) sending.

In the New Testament story, Jesus worked as change agent authorized by the God of Israel to proclaim a forthcoming innovation, a theocracy, the kingdom of God. Further, Jesus himself authorized change agents, namely, the twelve apostles sent by him during his career solely to the house of Israel (Matt 10:5) to influence an innovation decision in favor of Jesus' proclamation. In that story we also learn that Pharisee groups likewise authorized Israelite scribes to go on a mission on their behalf (mentioned in Matt 23), largely as apostles. Finally, in the book of Acts we find Jesus' former change agents, the Eleven, now serving as an agency commissioning others with various tasks in the service of proclaiming an innovation.

Paul was not sent by any such group. Rather, he insists that his authorization and commission came from the God of Israel alone, through an altered states-of-consciousness experience (Gal 1:11-12). In this he was just like Jesus and John the Baptist, both authorized to proclaim God's good news to Israel through altered states-of-consciousness experiences. Since these change agents were not sponsored or authorized by any observable change agency, they had to face questions of authorization or authority by those who inquired about or rejected the innovation. ("By what authority are you doing these things, or who gave you this authority to do them?" [Mark 11:27-33] and parallels for Jesus and John; see John 7:17-18).

Paul, as well as Jesus and John the Baptist, were such socially unauthorized change agents who communicated information about an innovation and sought to influence innovation decisions in a direction deemed desirable by them in terms of their experience of the God of Israel. They insisted that the God of Israel was the change agency behind their proclamation and the explanations that they offered on the basis of their experience of God. As with John the Baptist and Jesus before him, the urgency that Paul intimates in his activities derives from the charge he had received from the change agency, the God of Israel.

This feature underscores the conviction of early Jesus group-members that the "founder" of both the task and the coalition inaugurated by Jesus as well as of the post-resurrection Jesus groups was none other than the God of Israel. The God of Israel founded "Christianity." The innovation that Jesus proclaimed was a forthcoming Israelite theocracy or the kingdom of heaven ("heaven" was a surrogate or substitute name for "God"). Paul traveled to Greco-Roman cities with Israelite minority populations along the northeastern Mediterranean. The innovation that he proclaimed to his fellow Israelites was that the God of Israel raised Jesus from the dead, thus revealing Jesus to be Israel's Messiah (Christ) and cosmic Lord, with a view to the forthcoming Israelite theocracy (1 Thess). According to the New Testament witness, then, the founder or change agency of Jesus groups and their ideology or belief system was God, the God of Israel. God's directly authorized change agents, such as John the Baptist, Jesus, and Paul, all functioned for the same change agency, the God of Israel. To shift the thrust from the agency to the agent is to displace the beliefs of early Jesus groups, groups that emerge after Emperor Constantine in AD 313 as "Christendom."

As change agent for the God of Israel (change agency), Paul had to make known and then spell out the significance and ramification of the innovation inaugurated by the change agency (God of Israel). His target audience was Israelites found "among the Gentiles." And since all the proofs presented in his own and collaborative letters are based on the sacred writings of Israel, it is clear that only Israelites would be convinced by such arguments. In other words, Paul's actual target audience was Israelites alone. If this sounds odd, think of someone approaching you or another American to convert and do God's will while basing all his arguments on the Avesta. First of all, most Americans would not know what the Avesta is (the sacred books of the Parsi, the ancient Persian Magi). And second, those writings would hardly be considered authoritative by Americans so as to clinch an argument about the truth of a change agent's contentions. What the Avesta is to Americans, so Israel's Torah was to non-Israelites (that is, Gentiles) in the first-century Mediterranean. Actually, Paul showed no interest in non-Israelites at all. He had no Gospel for them.

As change agent to Israelite minorities in Greco-Roman cities such as Thessalonika or Corinth or Philippi, Paul invariably had the following seven tasks, occurring in no fixed order apart from the first and last steps. We know this because these tasks are part of what every and any change agent seeking success in communicating an innovation had to do.

Change Agent Tasks

First Step	Any Order	Final Step
1. Develop Need to Change	2. Information-Exchange Relationship 3. Diagnose Problems 4. Create Intent to Change 5. Translate Intent into Action 6. Stabilize and Prevent Discontinuance	7. Terminate Relationship

We will briefly consider each of these steps in turn.

STEP 1: DEVELOP NEED TO CHANGE

First of all, Paul had to develop a need for change and convince prospective clients of their need to adopt this Israelite innovation. Paul describes this phase of his activity as "proclaiming the gospel of God" to his fellow Israelites. The book of Acts presents ideal scenarios of how Paul performed this initial function in terms of a travel story punctuated by geographical stopovers. When Paul went into a town with an Israelite minority, he would speak to his fellow Israelites, as was the usual custom with a visiting fellow ingroup member. He would tell them of what the God of Israel, the God of their ancestors, had recently done for Israelites in Judea by raising a holy man and prophet from the dead, a holy man and prophet named Jesus from Nazareth in Galilee. This Jesus, given that the God of Israel raised him from the dead, will be Israel's forthcoming Messiah, and his messianic activity would lead to the establishment of a theocracy in Israel. Given what God had done to him, this Jesus must also be some sort of special personage, worthy of being treated as a cosmic Lord in the realm of God.

In these synagogues or gatherings, some members found what Paul said convincing and relevant. These would be the innovators and first adopters who requested Paul to tell them more. They constituted a smattering or at least a splintering of relatively small synagogue groups or gatherings in a given city. The traditionalists among them did not accept what Paul had to say. In their view, while Paul's proclamation sounded wonderful for Israelites in Judea, Perea, and Galilee, here in the larger cities of the Mediterranean, it could only lead to difficulties with their townmates and perhaps further difficulties with Romans, for whom Judea was a piece of a province. When some in their groups adopted the innovation, the result was that Israelite traditionalists developed a grievance against Paul for splitting up their community. At times the writer of the book of Acts describes how a grievance against Paul developed into a conflict, and eventually into a dispute. A grievance is the perception of a person or group being injured by another; a conflict is hostile interaction between two persons or groups, while a dispute involves a third party in some conflict. Consider this sequence in Acts 17:1-9:

> Now when they had passed through Amphipolis and Apollonia, they came to Thessalonica, where there was a synagogue of the [Judeans]. And Paul went in, as was his custom, and for three weeks he argued with them from the scriptures, explaining and proving that it was necessary for the Christ to suffer and to rise from the dead, and saying, "This Jesus, whom I proclaim to you, is the Christ." And some of them were persuaded, and joined Paul and Silas; as did a great many of the devout Greeks and not a few of the leading women. But the [Judeans] were jealous, and taking some wicked fellows of the rabble, they gathered a crowd, set the city in an uproar, and attacked the house of Jason, seeking to bring them out to the people. And when they could not find them, they dragged Jason and some of the brethren before the city authorities, crying, "These men who have turned the world upside down have come here also, and Jason has received them; and they are all acting against the decrees of Caesar, saying that there is another king, Jesus." And the people and the city authorities were disturbed when they heard this. And when they had taken security from Jason and the rest, they let them go.

In Luke's description, after Paul's proclamation and explanation, some synagogue members with a grievance against Paul developed their grievance into a conflict. They pushed the conflict into a dispute, with city government members moving into the fray. These cities were small (seven to thirty thousand), and the disputes took place in the Israelite sections of those small cities. The gossip network would spread information about the conflict.[4] Since the aggrieved parties were well established, as the conflict bubbled over and as gossip spread, notice of the conflict soon spread to the authorities of the city.

The result was that Paul would have to leave or face the consequence. He left and in his place one or another of the local innovators took over the small Jesus group that accepted Paul's gospel of God. These people faced further difficulties with the aggrieved group, with whom they differed. These innovators and first adopters had to stand up to the local aggrieved synagogue members. The outcome, of course, was a sort of conflict, with social pressure to return to the synagogue. In Greek, this social pressure was called *thlipsis,* a word often poorly translated as "persecution" (see Rom 5:3; 8:35; 12:12; 2 Cor 1:4, 8; 6:4; Phil 1:17; 4:14; 1 Thess 1:6; 3:3, 7). Most of the time this *thlipsis* involved shunning, banning, negative gossip, and reports to the government officials that these people looked forward to a new political order or theocracy in Judea—something that would not sit well with Romans and their vision of imperial order. But this is often not explicitly spelled out, only alluded to.

Step 2: Information-Exchange Relationship

The second step for a change agent is to establish an information-exchange relationship with the innovators and early adopters of the innovation. This is precisely the stage at which Paul's letter-writing activity and coworkers fit in. All of Paul's letters apart from Romans are premised on a relationship entailing information exchange with persons who have accepted the innovation proclaimed by Paul to some extent. It is also with a view to information exchange that Paul sends his associates (1 Cor 4:19; 16:10; Phil 2:19, 22; 1 Thess 3:26). Timothy is the most mentioned associate in this task. And since he is mentioned as being at work in the very first Pauline letter (1 Thess), one may presume that he was an early adopter of the innovation proclaimed by Paul as well as an opinion leader in his home city. Timothy's participation in developing an information-exchange relation with persons in Pauline Jesus groups embraced the following three areas: to diagnose problems, to create intent to change, and to prevent discontinuance. Timothy, as well as Paul and Paul's other coworkers, were to fulfill these tasks. While these tasks did not and need not occur in any fixed sequence, we will consider them in the order presented in the chart above (p. 55).

STEP 3: DIAGNOSE PROBLEMS

The information-exchange relationship between Paul and Timothy and their clients dealt with, among other things, the diagnosis of their clients' problems arising from the innovation proclaimed by Paul and Timothy. This feature is quite obvious in all the Pauline letters. For example, in 1 Thessalonians there are problems concerning order in the Jesus-group gathering (1 Thess 4:9-12); concerning recently deceased Jesus-group members (1 Thess 4:13-18); concerning the time of the coming of Jesus in power (*parousia*—1 Thess 5:1-11).

It is significant to note that it was through Timothy that many of these problems were resolved in the Jesus group of Thessalonika (1 Thess 3:2-6). The solution to these problems described in the first letter to the Thessalonians was the work of Paul, Silvanus, and Timothy. In 1 Corinthians there were the problems reported by Chloe's people and those about which some Corinthians wrote to Paul concerning marriage and having children (1 Cor 7:1-38); concerning food offered before images of the deceased (1 Cor 8:1–11:1); concerning behavior in celebrating the Lord's Supper (1 Cor 11:17-34); concerning gifts of the Spirit (1 Cor 12:1–14:40); and concerning the resurrection of the dead (1 Cor 15:1-58). Once more Paul states that he sent Timothy to resolve these problems (1 Cor 4:17).

STEP 4: CREATE INTENT TO CHANGE

While the Pauline letters and reference to the Pauline team describe an information-exchange relationship focused on diagnosing problems raised by the innovation proclaimed by Paul, they also deal with the need to turn the information the clients have presumably accepted into the firm intention to change. The change involved was not a conversion in our sense of the term. It would be totally anachronistic to believe that Israelites were asked to convert to Christianity by Paul. In fact, no Israelite was asked to convert to Christianity because there was no "Christianity."

What Paul and Timothy sought was for their fellow Israelites to continue in their obedience to the God of Israel. The Gospel they proclaimed was about the recent activity of Israel's ancestral God. Hence what Paul and his change agents sought was not conversion but continued obedience to the will of the God of Israel. As the God of Israel was once revealed to Moses in a burning Bush (read Exodus 3), so now the God of Israel reveals himself in the death and resurrection of Jesus. And just as God revealed his name to Moses as "I AM WHO I AM," (Exod 3:14), so now God again reveals his name as "He who raised Christ Jesus from the dead" (Rom 4:24; 8:11). Of course, this is the ancestral God of Israel, the God of Abraham, Isaac, and Jacob. The information-exchange relationship set up by Paul and associates in terms of cowritten letters and associates on site always involves encouraging clients to persevere in the decision they had made to obey the God of Israel by joining the Jesus group. Such encouragement points to supporting the clients' intent to change. Again, this is a feature common in the communication of innovation.

STEP 5: TRANSLATE INTENT INTO ACTION

Change agents always want their clients to translate their intent to change into action. For Paul and his associates, proof of this translation of intent into action is summed up in the word "love" coupled with doing. In the first-century Mediterranean, "love" was an attitude of group attachment, of attachment to one's fellow Jesus-group members, a sense of being bonded with the group. This love may or may not be accompanied by feelings of affection. However, this sense of attachment to the group and its members has to be coupled with actions, with doing, with group support. The Pauline writings, at the close of all of their exhortations, always call to action, to do what is suggested in the exhortations, to actually behave accordingly (read 1 Thess 5:12-24; 1 Cor 13:1-14; 2 Cor 13:11; Gal 6:1-10; Phil 4:2-9).

STEP 6: STABILIZE AND PREVENT DISCONTINUANCE

Some of those who initially adopt some innovation eventually come to discontinue the innovation. So change agents such as Paul and Timothy have to stabilize adoption and prevent discontinuance. The letter to the Galatians, written by Paul alone, is an example of his urging his clients not to discontinue in favor of an alternative version of the innovation. Paul calls such alternate versions "another" or "different" or "contrary" gospel (Gal 1:6-9). Yet all the Pauline letters in one way or another urge his clients to continue in the innovation that Paul and the Pauline team proclaimed.

STEP 7: TERMINATE RELATIONSHIP

When a client group adopts an innovation in some stable way, the change agent's goal is to achieve a terminal relationship. Once a Jesus group is set up and functioning on its own, a change agent like Paul and his associates, like Timothy, must move on. In Paul's case we have evidence of his intent to move on in his letter to the Romans. Since Paul can say that "from Jerusalem and as far round as Illyricum I have fully preached the gospel of Christ" (Rom 15:19), he is ready to move on: "I no longer have any room for work in these regions" (Rom 15:23).

Who took Paul's place in the Jesus groups he founded? First- and second-generation Jesus-group change agents were succeeded by local central personages, at times a board of elders (*presbyteroi*), at others by a single central person ("supervisor"). Evidence of such central persons is plentiful from the documents dating to the third generation after Paul, the book of Acts and especially the letters to Timothy and Titus. The supervisors (*episkopoi*, pronounced "bishops" in later English) are actually successors of these Jesus-group change agents, the "traveling apostles" of Acts. According to the story in Acts, since the official twelve witnesses to all that Jesus said and did essentially stayed in Jerusalem and vicinity and did not found churches, they did not have successors. In fact, witnesses do not have successors in their role as witnesses. However, much later tradition held that they did travel and work as change agents with successors. Think of Saint Peter having a successor in Rome, Saint James in Spain (Compostella), Saint Thomas in India, or even Saint Andrew in Scotland. In this later tradition, the Twelve traveled to the ends of the earth, a requirement for Jesus' return (Mark 13:10: "The gospel must first be preached to all nations").

The point here is that Paul and the Pauline team, as change agents, would expect to achieve a terminal relationship with the groups they founded after their change-agent task was completed. The third-generation letter to Timothy depicts Paul's coworker as such a successor to Paul resident in Ephesus. And tradition will remember Timothy as bishop of Ephesus.

These seven foregoing features mark Paul's "apostolate to [Israelites among] the Gentiles." They also set the boundaries for Timothy's activities. As coworker and cowriter, Timothy functioned as an aide to Paul. References in the Pauline letters describe Timothy as active in the tasks of maintaining an information-exchange relationship with the Jesus groups founded by Paul. His reports to Paul indicate that he diagnosed the problems that arose in those groups as they attempted to assimilate Paul's gospel of God, to translate this Gospel into appropriate social forms and behaviors, as well as to prevent discontinuance of the innovation.

Choosing Coworkers

As a general rule, change agents use opinion leaders in a social system as their lieutenants in diffusion campaigns. This means that the people whom Paul chose as coworkers, such as Timothy or Silvanus or Titus, were opinion leaders in one or another Jesus group founded by Paul. An opinion leader is an individual who is able to influence the attitudes and/or behavior of others informally and in a desired way with relative frequency. Opinion leaders foster obedience to the demands of the innovation and allay dissonance. These opinion leaders have no formal authority. As Paul frequently notes, he is *the* authority in the Jesus groups he founded.

Why would Paul choose the coworkers that he did? Why would Paul choose Timothy, for example? Paul's mode of proclaiming his gospel of God was a form of interpersonal communication that occurred horizontally, that is, to fellow Israelites. Yet, as he insists, he is an apostle, one who had seen the resurrected Jesus, and this put him higher in the ingroup status system of Jesus groups. It also put him at a certain disadvantage relative to the members of the groups he founded. After all, he had what Romans called *auctoritas*, the socially recognized ability to control the behavior of others.

To assist in effective communication, Paul chose aides or coworkers from the ranks of opinion leaders, who shared the same status as other innovators in the group. We know from cross-cultural studies that opinion leaders conform to the norms of their local social system.[5] They represent the system's norms and values. While they are persons of significant local ingroup status, they usually are similar in certain attributes, such as cultural beliefs, levels of being informed, general social status, and the like. Opinion leaders usually have social competencies like gregariousness, sociability, interpersonal competence, age. Since they have much in common with others in their group, they are technically labeled "homophilous," having very similar social traits.

A coworker's task was to maintain contact with clients to influence their innovation decisions. These coworkers were usually much like with the average client ("homophilous"). In this way they provided one means of bridging the difference gap frequently found between an apostle like Paul and his client audience. Paul's aides were less than the fully "professional" change agent he was. His change-agent task was his life, his profession. But Paul's coworkers were closer to the ingroup members of the Jesus-group system that they served. In the case of the proclamation of the Gospel, Paul's aides perhaps were not as adept or expert in knowledge and use of Israel's sacred scriptures, for example. But they made up for their lower degree of technical expertise through their greater social expertness. Thus the selection of coworkers according to their interpersonal competence and personal acquaintance with the Hellenistic client system served to minimize the social distance between the change-agent system of the Jerusalemite Jesus group (James, Peter, and John, for example) and the client system of Israelites living in the Hellenistic Mediterranean. Once Paul's proclamation was accepted, a homophilous coworker like Timothy often halved the social distance between a change agent like Paul and his designated client population, which consisted of Israelites resident among a non-Israelite majority.

What were Paul's client populations like? What sort of Israelites did Paul approach? Change agents authorized by human agencies can readily prove their authorization and presume on the social status and power of their verifiable change agency. For example, a change agent authorized by an emperor, a local king, a temple priesthood, or a city council could readily approach elites of all sorts, gaining access in the name of the authorizing agency.[6] But change agents such as Paul (or John the Baptist or Jesus), without authorization by some verifiable human change agency, could not rely directly on a display of the social status and power of the God of Israel. It would be shameful to invoke divine power on one's own behalf in a procedure looking much like magic (see Acts 8:18-19).

What this meant for social interaction is that such divinely authorized change agents did not take a top-down, vertical approach to their fellows, but rather a horizontal approach. In the case of Jesus, note the saying: "But blessed are your eyes, for they see, and your ears, for they hear. Truly, I say to you, many prophets and righteous men longed to see what you see, and did not see it, and to hear what you hear, and did not hear it." (Matt 13:16-17). Revelations were meant for prophets and righteous men, not for ordinary people. But Jesus congratulates his audience of ordinary people on their experience of God's revelation. His is an audience of a social status similar to his own. The same is true for Paul. Paul approached persons similar to himself or his coworkers, those with whom they shared certain attributes, such as beliefs, education, social status, and the like. On the other hand, since Paul's change agency was not a human one, he would not, and did not, approach prospective clients who were very different, such as elites or non-Israelites. And neither did Jesus. Such prospective clients would be too different in attributes such as beliefs, education, social status, and the like.

Paul's change agency and its focus offer another reason to explain why Paul and the Pauline team did not approach non-Israelites. The innovation communicated by Paul and associates largely involved the transfer of information and ideas. Now cross-cultural studies have demonstrated that the transfer of information and ideas in a system, even if it is slow, takes place most frequently and more effectively between individuals who are alike. Paul's audiences were fellow Israelites living in Israelite enclaves, where they formed minority population segments in Greco-Roman *poleis*. Paul does not go "to the circumcision," where Israelites would form substantial segments of the population (e.g., Jerusalem, Alexandria, Antioch, Damascus, some North African cities, and the like).

Homophilous communication is rather slow and seems characteristic of the spread of Jesus groups. Historians tell us that 220 Jesus-group bishops attended Constantine's Council of Nicea, a meeting to which he summoned all Jesus-group bishops in AD 325.[7] Anthropologists tell us that in a society without mass media of communication, the largest network a person can maintain is 4,000 people.[8] Hence the number of Jesus-group members after three hundred years was about

880,000. This annual growth rate of 2.5 percent points to the outcome of homophilous communication.

Paul's Political Message
for His Israelite Clients

The Israelite innovation communicated by Paul and associates to Israelite groups located in non-Israelite–majority cities of the northeastern Mediterranean was a piece of radically new political-religious news. The God of Israel was on the verge of instituting an Israelite theocracy. The harbinger of this event was the act by which this God raised a person named Jesus from the dead, thus constituting him Israel's forthcoming Messiah and Lord—all with a view to the forthcoming theocracy. This was the sum and substance of Paul's proclamation to his audience, Israelites living in non-Israelite–majority cities. Why would any Israelite bother believing this news? What did it offer that Israelites outside of Palestine did not already have?

As we have previously noted, people of the first-century Mediterranean were not individualistic, seeking their personal salvation in some far-off sky, even with the God of Israel; rather they were collectivistic persons. That means that the integrity and well-being of the group with which they were affiliated was far more important than personal well-being coming from individual self-reliance. And the group with which all Israelites were affiliated was, of course, the house of Israel, centered in Jerusalem and its sacred temple. The Romans invaded Palestine in the days of the general Pompei (on our universal calendar, 63 BC), with a view to "civilizing" the barbarians (Judeans) of the region. The Romans believed that their task from the gods was to civilize, that is, bring Hellenistic or Greek values, outlooks, and behaviors along with Roman order. In return for the favor of civilizing barbarians, the Romans required tax payments.

Of course, this was not something Israelites readily accepted. In Judea, for example, consider the following of persons attracted by the several messianic claimants and their hopes of a theocracy in the period before Jesus (see Acts 5:36 about a certain revolutionary named Theudas, d. AD 44, or 5:37 about Judas the Galilean, another revolutionary, who died in AD 6). During this period the house of Israel was ruled by Israelite kings largely schooled in Rome: Herod the Great over all Israel, and then his sons Archaelaus over Judea, Samaria, and Idumea; Herod Antipas over Galilee and Perea; and Philip over the region east and north of the Sea of Galilee. Archaelaus proved incompetent by Roman standards and so was replaced by a Roman procurator or prefect for Judea, Samaria, and Idumea. Herod Antipas ruled Galilee during the period of Jesus' prophetic activity there. Israelite elites, collaborators with the Romans, took advantage of the situation by taking more and more land from Galilean small holders, while Romans extorted taxes. The result was that very many Galileans were reduced to a rather penurious existence. It was in such a context that Jesus proclaimed the forthcoming kingdom of God, a political-religious social entity that would restore Israel's place in the world.[9]

What the Romans and collaborating Israelite elite had done was to totally humiliate the house of Israel. The coming of the kingdom of God would restore their honor. In the New Testament period, the word "redemption" meant restoring the honor of a social group that had been dishonored. Honor was a core value in the Mediterranean world; it was a claim to worth and having others recognize and acknowledge that worth. Israel in the first century was located in the Roman province of Palestine, with many thousands of Israelites located as minorities in non-Israelite–majority cities. To exist as a conquered people, as a minority people living among a non-Israelite majority, was a situation of permanent dishonor. Redemption effected by the God of Israel would look to restoring the honor of all Israel, of Israel among all nations (Matt 28:19). Jesus' followers perceived God working in Jesus' being raised as the beginning of the restoration of honor. Jesus' being raised from the dead by the God of Israel pointed to the coming of the kingdom of God rather soon.

Since "redemption" meant the restoration of the honor of a family or group, a redeemer was the person who restored that honor. The hymns cited in the first two chapters of Luke's Gospel are explicit statements in this regard. Mary's *Magnificat* in Luke 1:46-55 and Zechariah's *Benedictus* in Luke 1:68-79 are clearly political-religious psalms. Even Simeon's song ends with a statement of Jesus' coming "for glory to your people Israel" (Luke 2:34); glory refers to honor shown and acknowledged by others. Paul makes explicit mention of this restored honor in 1 Cor 1:30; Gal 3:13; 4:5; Rom 3:24; 8:23, although the theme is implicit in his whole assessment of the work of Christ Jesus. Hence to understand why anybody among Paul's fellow Israelites would accept his gospel of God, one must realize that the problem for Israel in the first-century Mediterranean was Israel's dishonored state, at least in the perception of the Israelites whom Paul addressed.

Conclusion

In time, the ramifications of Paul's gospel of God would become incorporated into the regular activities of the various Jesus groups that Paul and his team had founded. The innovation would lose its separate identity. And with this, the innovation process in a community was complete. Communal members no longer thought of the innovation as a new idea. However, as we find from the Pauline writings, it seems that routine functioning was not fully in place during the period of Paul and Timothy, perhaps not at all in the first few Pauline generations. These were periods of further filling out, for example, in the second-generation writings called the second letter to the Thessalonians and third Pauline-generation concerns in the letters to the Colossians and to Timothy and Titus. It seems that the general third Pauline-generation documents called Ephesians and Hebrews looked to the concerns of minority Gentiles (Ephesians) and Judeans (Hebrews) in prevalently Pauline Israelite Greek communities.

The letter to the Romans does not fit into this model of Paul's change-agency activity and group-innovation adoption. The reason for this is that Romans is really about travel arrangements. In the process of requesting hospitality, Paul wants to show Jesus-group members in Rome (none of whom seem to be Romans) that he has much in common with them, and if there is anything they heard about him that was negative in their estimation, it really was not true or not what he said or not what he meant. So with the letter he makes travel arrangements and intends to rectify the distorted gossip they may have heard about him.

What the models that we have presented here underscore is that while the proclamation and acceptance of the gospel of God was fundamental, subsequently it was not Paul's theology or Timothy's teaching that was of interest to their fellow Jesus-group Israelites. Rather it was the interpersonal exchange relationship that their letters and physical presence were meant to maintain, with a view to group stability. To focus on Paul's theology, which was also Timothy's, rather than on the social inter-relationship between the change agent, change-agent aide, and their clients is to miss the thrust of the behavior called the diffusion of innovation.

CHAPTER 4

Specifics about Timothy: Paul's Cowriter and Coworker

I n the previous chapters we considered several significant
social-system structures that can prove useful for developing an appreciation of the first-century Eastern Mediterranean Israelite, Paul's coworker and cowriter, Timothy. The
information is stereotypical and generic, applicable to any number of persons in Mediterranean societies of the time, as well as
to specific Israelite groups. The specific features of any individual
person cannot be concluded from such generic information, but
the information does enable an American reader to realize, to
some extent, some fundamental differences between first-century
Mediterranean persons and people in the United States today.
However, there are some primary sources dealing with Timothy
that provide specific, contemporary information about him.
These are the letters that Paul wrote with the collaboration of
Timothy as well as others. In this chapter we will consider the
references to Timothy in these letters.

Timothy collaborated in the writing of four letters with Paul.
These include a letter to the Thessalonians, the first written docu-
ment among early Jesus-group writings, then letters to the
Corinthians (now clustered in 2 Corinthians), to the Philippians,

and to Philemon. He also figures prominently in other letters (notably 1 Corinthians) in his function as coworker or change-agent aide.

The Letter of Paul, Silvanus, and Timothy to the Thessalonians

A reading of what is called the first letter to the Thessalonians indicates that it was written after Timothy visited the Jesus-group in the city of Thessalonica, then returned to Paul and Silvanus with the news that the Gospel innovation they had proclaimed there had taken root, as evidenced by the behavior and attitudes of the Thessalonians. This news, of course, relieved Paul's anxiety, since his honor was tightly bound up with the success of his change-agent tasks. This letter has two main parts. The first part deals with the relationship between the change agents in general and the Jesus group they formed (1 Thess 1:2–3:13), and the second part presents some pertinent directives and exhortations (1 Thess 4:1–5:24). The letter opens as follows:

> Paul, Silvanus, and Timothy, to the church of the Thessalonians in God the Father and the Lord Jesus Christ: Grace to you and peace. (1 Thess 1:1)

This is a typical opening formula of a Hellenistic letter. The opening formula consisted of the name of the sender(s), then the addressee(s), and a greeting. These three elements are called a superscription (or prescript). This formula is to be found in all of the letters that Timothy has collaboratively written, but with distinctive alterations. Here these Jesus-group change-agents add an ingroup description of Thessalonian Jesus groups as being "in God the Father and the Lord Jesus Christ." This expansion of the addressee segment of the Hellenistic letter is a first indication of the theological outlook behind Paul's proclamation of the kingdom of God, which was Timothy's theology as well.

The senders here are Paul, Silvanus, and Timothy, a change-agent team. Their task, as we learn from the rest of the letter, was to communicate the innovation wrought by the God of Israel in raising Jesus from the dead with a view to a new political-religious system for Israel. The sequence of names in this superscription has to do with precedence, with Paul first, Silvanus second, and Timothy third. This indicates that Silvanus joined Paul before Timothy did (the third Pauline-generation writer of the Acts of the Apostles knew this; see Acts 15:40). On the other hand, all three are listed as senders of the letter. This indicates they were cowriters in a collectivistic social context. From a later Christian perspective, "authorship" of a canonical biblical writing is considered inspired by God, with inspiration being a Spirit-inspired charisma. Sacred writers were inspired by God to write what they did. This, of course, means that along with Paul, Silvanus and Timothy likewise belong to the ranks of those ancient sacred writers in the Jesus tradition.

The names of the senders are Greek, pointing to civilized persons. In the first century AD there was no "Greece" in our sense of the word. "Greek" was a status, not a reference to origin.[1] To be a Greek basically meant to be Hellenized, a synonym for "civilized." The opposite of "Greek" was "barbarian, uncivilized." Along with a number of values, the common Greek language of the period was the language used by civilized people in the Mediterranean in the first century AD. And Greek was the language of the New Testament.

The word "church" translates the Greek *ekklēsia*, a much-used term found here for the first time in Jesus-group writings. It is a word taken from the civilized Greek vocabulary to refer to a gathering of the entitled residents of a *polis*, the Greek term for the larger organized settlement usually translated "city." Hence it refers to a gathering of citizens of a city (the word "citizen" referred solely to such "cities"; there was no national citizenship before the nineteenth century); citizens had the privilege of deciding matters of significance to the city and the obligation to support what was of significance to the city.

Moreover, *ekklēsia* was used in the Greek (hence civilized) version of Israel's sacred Scriptures, called "the Septuagint" (a Latin word meaning the number LXX, or 70, deriving from a legend according to which the Greek version of Israel's sacred writings was completed overnight by seventy learned scribes). In the Septuagint the word *ekklēsia* translated the Hebrew word *qahal*, which referred to those summoned or called by the God of Israel in the wilderness to serve God in the folkloric story of the Exodus and God's constituting the people of Israel. Significantly, Paul now sees the gathering of Jesus-group members as God's new summoned people, the *ekklēsia* of the God of Israel. In this way the term serves as a label providing group members with social identity, identifying them as a new Israel of a new Exodus covenant, and distinguishing them from their proximate, conflicting outgroup, the Judean *synagōgē*, a general Greek term also meaning "gathering," used by Israelites for their meetings.

Since the word "church" today refers to institutional Christianity, the locally gathered members of this institution, as well as the buildings in which Christians meet, its use in modern translations of the New Testament is rather anachronistic and misleading. Most scholars sensitive to social context prefer dropping the translation "church" in favor of "gathering" or "assembly." This "gathering of those called by God" in Thessalonika form a Jesus group. These Jesus groups consisted of people who shared faith in the God of Israel and what that God did in the raising of Jesus from the dead, with hope in a forthcoming kingdom of God.

The greeting describes the gathering of the Thessalonian Jesus-group members as "in God the Father." Paul's perspectives belong essentially to political religion, because the kingdom of God that he proclaims is a political-religious reality. This is a point that nearly all Bible scholars, professional and non-professional, totally overlook. In point of fact, to proclaim the kingdom of God is an expressly political statement. Any kingdom of God is a theocracy (think of the Islamic republic of Iran, a theocracy). Modern believers often take the kingdom of God to be someplace in the sky, an equivalent of heaven, hence invisible and available to the souls of the departed. Not so in antiquity. Perhaps this point needs some clarification.

In contemporary Western societies, religion is a social institution separate from other institutions such as kinship or family, economics, and government. Each of these institutions is actually a phase of social life in rather fixed form. Each is studied separately in various academic departments of a college or university. But such a separation of social institutions occurred in European history only in the eighteenth century. Separation of bank/economics and government/state was conceived of by Adam Smith (1776), while the separation of the institutional church and government was the outcome of the Enlightenment and the French Revolution. Since these separations occurred in the eighteenth century, church and state, as well as bank and state, were not separate earlier. Consider the observation of Paul's contemporary Philo, an Israelite philosopher and theologian who lived in the Israelite quarter of ancient Alexandria: "There are two types of organized communities (*poleis*): the larger and the smaller. The larger ones are called 'cities' (Greek: *astē*) and the smaller ones 'households' (Greek: *oikiai*)" (*Special Laws* 3.169). During the time of Jesus and Paul and Timothy, there were only two social institutions of note and concern to people: government or politics and kinship or family. Religion and economics were substantive institutions embedded in government (political religion and political economy) and in kinship (domestic religion and domestic economy).

What this means is that the activity of the Pauline change-agent team was about proclaiming a forthcoming political religion, a theocracy for Israelites. Their activity was a political-religious activity. More specifically, the Jesus groups organized by the Pauline team among Israelites in majority non-Israelite cities were fictive kin groups with a political-religious ideology. Such a structure is typical of a larger political unit composed of tribes. The tribes were kinship groups that belonged to an overarching political-religious unit. This unit had the God of Israel as supreme, with the resurrected Jesus as Lord. As fictive kin groups, the roles, statuses, and goals in these Jesus groups would derive from the prevailing kin groups' structures.

Timothy was a "brother" in the ingroup, while in their kinship-like relations, Paul was his "father" and he a beloved "child." The relationship between Paul and Timothy would be like that of a father with his adult son. While the Jesus group was based on faith and profession of a political-religious sort, the structure of the group was like that of a fictive kin group, of brothers and sisters in Christ. Of primary importance for group identity was group adherence rooted in the practical behavior of ingroup members toward one another. This is what "love" was about. As fictive kin groups, Jesus groups awaited God's founding of a kingdom in Israel. At that time the fictive kin groups would become part of an overarching political entity.

Political religions all have their theology. "Theology" here means God-focused and God-motivated reasoning, with God as the main actor in Jesus-group formation, support, and activity. It is important to note that in Pauline writings the word "God" invariably meant the God of Israel. After all, these writings come from a world where "there are many 'gods' and many 'lords'— yet for us there is one God, the Father, from whom are all things and for whom we exist, and one Lord, Jesus Christ, through whom are all things and through whom we exist" (1 Cor 8:5-6). The co-senders of this letter view the God of Israel as "Father," a word borrowed from the kinship institution and often used in the kin-like relationship of social superior to inferior called patronage. The God of Israel is most often described as "Father" or patron of the gathering summoned by God.

The role of "the Lord Jesus Christ" is that of intermediary, broker, go-between, between God and Jesus groups. Jesus' titles here are a mixture of Greek and Judean, that is, civilized and barbarian. The title "Lord" refers to Jesus as endowed with power, while "Christ" refers to Jesus as Israel's Messiah.

"Lord" (Greek: *kyrios*; Latin: *dominus*; Semitic: *adon* or *baal*) in the Hellenistic world meant a person having the most complete power over other persons and things. The lord is the absolute owner of all persons and things in his domain. He is a person who has the power to dispose of persons and things as he likes and who holds this power by a title recognized as valid (either by ad hoc force, custom, or law). This is lordship (Greek: *kyriotēs*, Latin: *dominium*). The lord was entitled to use any thing or person that was his, to enjoy all their products or properties, and to consume entirely whatever was capable of consumption. Given the perception that Jesus was with the God of Israel in the sky, to call Jesus "Lord" meant that he wielded supreme cosmic dominion, after God. Significantly, in this letter to the Thessalonians, the title "Lord" is the main title for Jesus, used twenty-four times (with article: 1:3, 6, 8; 2:15, 19; 3:11, 12, 13; 4:3, 15, 16, 17; 5:9, 23, 27, 28; without article: 1:1; 4:6, 15, 17; 5:2 and in the phrase "in the Lord" in 3:8; 4:1; 5:12). Given the fact that Paul's gospel is ultimately about a forthcoming Israelite theocracy (kingdom of God, 2:21), it is noteworthy that the reigning emperor, Claudius, likewise bore the title "lord." The underlying clash of political-religious ideologies is not far below the surface of social interactions.

"Christ" (Greek: *christos*; Semitic: *mashiah*) is an Israelite word referring to a person chosen by the God of Israel to be his vicegerent on behalf of the people Israel. This person may be an Israelite or a non-Israelite (for example, the Persian king Cyrus called Israel's messiah in Isa 45:1). The term literally means "anointed" because Israel's significant elite officeholders (priest, king, official prophet) took office by having oil poured on their heads. They were thus "oiled in" just as U.S. officials are "sworn in" by oath with their hand on the Bible. Of course, the process of pouring oil on a person symbolized the pouring in/on of power. It is a very small step to see how a person upon whom God's Wind or Spirit was poured was likewise "anointed" (as in Luke 4:18, following Isa 61:1). In first-century assessments, oil, water, fire, and wind were all liquids; people could be "anointed" with them as they could be dipped, that is "baptized," in them (see Matt 3:11; Luke 3:16).

Some scholars hold that the gathering of Jesus-group members in Thessalonika (and elsewhere) probably took place in an *insula*, or apartment-type building, since these first Thessalonian group members were low-status non-elites.[2] However, cross-cultural studies indicate that innovators and first adopters of innovations are rarely low-status persons. They presumably were of the same social level as their fellow Israelites in Thessalonika. While they surely did not belong to the 2 percent elites of this Roman provincial capital, and while they formed only a fraction of the Israelite community there, as innovators and first adopters they were socially rooted enough that they could bear any untoward reactions to their having adopted Paul's gospel of God.[3]

Thus from the superscription of this letter, we find that Timothy was a member of Paul's team, a change agent, a competent letter-composer, and a Jesus-group Israelite. This letter has more to say about Timothy's activities as Paul's coworker. In 2:17–3:13, the letter describes the situation that developed after Paul and his coworkers founded the Jesus group at Thessalonika. Like all change agents successful in developing a need for change, the adopting group quickly moved into an implementation phase, during which people tested the innovation and took it in a number of unexpected directions. To deal with such unexpected outcomes, a change agent had to establish an information-exchange relationship. The purpose of this information exchange was to diagnose problems, support the intent of clients to live out the change they accepted, and to stabilize and prevent discontinuance. Such an information-exchange relationship entailed renewed visits by either Paul or some fellow staff member or by letters. This letter, in fact, was itself a follow-up to Timothy's visit, a visit that served the process of building an information-exchange relationship.

During his visit, Timothy discovered problems from outside the Thessalonian Jesus group: "For you, brethren, became imitators of the churches of God in Christ Jesus which are in Judea; for you suffered the same things from your own countrymen as they did from the Judeans, who killed both the Lord Jesus and the prophets, and drove us out, and displease God and oppose all men" (2:14-15). The Pauline team expected that the Thessalonian Jesus-group members would be distressed due to the inevitable conflict that would emerge when their fellow Israelites expressed their grievance against them.

Such conflict was the experience of Jesus groups in Judea, and Paul himself had to deal with it in his own case. Undoubtedly the Thessalonian innovation adopters were harassed in a way to cause grief or social suffering to their former synagogue associates due to their adoption of the gospel of God. Such conflict led to strengthening the ingroup ties of the Jesus group over against fellow Israelites in the city. It served in the building of social identity as Jesus-group members. The social experience of persistent annoyance, coupled with pleas and importunities from their fellow Israelites, marked the temptation or loyalty test that Paul ascribes to the "tempter," that is, Satan (read 1 Thess 3:5).

While Paul personally desired to visit the Thessalonians once more (he says so in 2:17-20), perhaps he was not fully confident in the outcome of such a visit, so he and his coworkers sent one of his team, Timothy. As the cowriters note, the outcome of Timothy's visit was quite successful (3:1-10), so the senders conclude with further best wishes for divine favors on the Thessalonian Jesus group (3:11-13):

> Therefore when we could bear it no longer, we were willing to be left behind at Athens alone, and we sent Timothy, our brother and God's servant in the gospel of Christ, to establish you in your faith and to exhort you, that no one be moved by these afflictions. You yourselves know that this is to be our lot. For when we were with you, we told you beforehand that we were to suffer affliction; just as it has come to pass, and as you know. For this reason, when I could bear it no longer, I sent that I might know your faith, for fear that somehow the tempter had tempted you and that our labor would be in vain. But now that Timothy has come to us from you, and has brought us the good news of your faith and love and reported that you always

remember us kindly and long to see us, as we long to see
you—for this reason, brethren, in all our distress and
affliction we have been comforted about you through your
faith. (1 Thess 3:1-7)

In this passage, verses 1-5 form a unit, marked off by the phrase
"to bear it no longer."

Sending Timothy was a group decision. We further learn that
Timothy's relationship with his fellows was that of a brother
and coworker. Timothy brought information that diffused Paul's
anxieties, for the Thessalonians, in face of attacks by fellow
Israelites, have in fact persisted in the innovation they had
adopted, relying upon God (faith) and continuing in their
attachment to the ingroup (love) and still holding Paul in high
esteem.

In sum, Timothy was co-sender of the very first document of
the Jesus movement. He was a participant in stabilizing the
establishment of the Jesus group at Thessalonika.

The Letter of Paul and Sosthenes
to the Corinthians

The next letter in the Pauline collection to mention Timothy
is the first letter to the Corinthians. In that letter the co-senders
make reference to Timothy as being on his way to visit the Corinthians, presumably for the same purpose that he was sent to
visit the Thessalonians. The purpose was to diagnose problems
and stabilize the Jesus group while preventing discontinuance.
After offering his reflections on the change-agents task (1 Cor
4:1-13), Paul continues:

I do not write this to make you ashamed, but to admonish
you as my beloved children. For though you have countless
guides in Christ, you do not have many fathers. For I became your father in Christ Jesus through the gospel. I urge
you, then, be imitators of me. Therefore I sent to you Timothy, my beloved and faithful child in the Lord, to remind

> you of my ways in Christ, as I teach them everywhere in
> every church. Some are arrogant, as though I were not com-
> ing to you. But I will come to you soon, if the Lord wills,
> and I will find out not the talk of these arrogant people but
> their power. For the kingdom of God does not consist in
> talk but in power. What do you wish? Shall I come to you
> with a rod, or with love in a spirit of gentleness? (1 Cor
> 4:14-21)

While Paul says that he does not wish to shame the adherents
of the Corinthian cliques, he surely does so. We find out eventually why he does so: because they act arrogantly, therefore chal-
lenging Paul's honor and those of others in the group who are
not "wise." Every challenge requires a riposte, and this is Paul's.
And yet this is an ingroup interaction; hence the goal is not
simply to shame the other person but to mend ingroup relations.
As Paul notes, his real goal is to admonish his "beloved children." As initial change agent, the first to proclaim the gospel
of God to them, Paul is like their father, not like a guardian. A
guardian (Greek: *paidagogos*) was a person, often a slave, whose
task it was to accompany children and youths to and from their
place of learning and to supervise their conduct in general. It
was those who came after Paul who were like family guardians,
that is, the traveling prophets and teachers. "Ten thousand" is
"myriad" in Greek, the largest number word, like our million
or billion used to be. And so as a father, Paul would have his
children imitate him and not reinvent the innovation he proclaimed to them.

In pursuing his change-agent task, Paul uses a letter (1 Cor 5:9),
and then Timothy in place of a letter, to maintain the information-
exchange relation so necessary for the successful implementation
of an innovation. The problem faced by the Pauline team arose
through Corinthian reinventions that entailed changing or
modifying the innovation in the process of its adoption and
implementation. These changes may have derived from persons
in contact with Kephas or Apollo. The result was ingroup wran-
gling (see 1 Cor 1:10-17). In their adoption of Paul's gospel, the

Corinthians departed from what Paul believed was the proper implementation of the innovation he promoted. The existence of cliques in Corinth, along with the problems that arose among their group members (1 Cor 7–15), point to such changes and modifications to the mainline version of the innovation that was promoted by Paul and his change-agent team.

In Paul's diagnosis, the root of the problem was arrogance (1 Cor 4:18-19, and previously, v. 6; also 5:2). Arrogance is an exaggeration of one's own worth or importance in an overbearing manner. It is a claim to honor gone wild. The Corinthian presumptuous claims to wisdom (1 Cor 1:18-31) is an indication of such arrogance. In an honor and shame society, arrogance is always a challenge to the honor of persons higher in social standing. In context, the person challenged is Paul, God's authorized change agent. Some Corinthians were willing to challenge Paul's honor, since they did not believe that he would come to them again. Such a challenge is really folly, the letter argues, since if Paul should return as he hopes, the arrogant challenge will be deflated, and all involved will be utterly shamed.

What is implied in this interaction is the Roman value of *auctoritas*, "authority." Authority means the socially sanctioned ability to control the behavior of others. Authority usually derives from one's ascribed status, the status that group members believe one is entitled to. Like power, authority enables a person to have an effect on other people. And the forthcoming Israelite theocracy is about power, the power of God in and through Christ, already manifest in various altered states-of-consciousness phenomena, here called the gifts of the Spirit. So Paul tells the Corinthians to back down and let him exercise his authority with the gentleness of one attached to group members, that is, with love.

However, the notice at the close of the letter in 1 Cor 16:10 presumes that Timothy did not get there yet: "When Timothy comes, see that you put him at ease among you, for he is doing the work of the Lord, as I am." This means that Paul and Sosthenes sent this letter while Timothy was on his way. Paul notes this point at the close of the letter, where he gives his travel plans (1 Cor 16:5-11):

> I will visit you after passing through Macedonia, for I intend to pass through Macedonia, and perhaps I will stay with you or even spend the winter, so that you may speed me on my journey, wherever I go. For I do not want to see you now just in passing; I hope to spend some time with you, if the Lord permits. But I will stay in Ephesus until Pentecost, for a wide door for effective work has opened to me, and there are many adversaries. When Timothy comes, see that you put him at ease among you, for he is doing the work of the Lord, as I am. So let no one despise him. Speed him on his way in peace, that he may return to me; for I am expecting him with the brethren. (1 Cor 16:5-11)

Paul is not sure whether Timothy, who obviously is not with him in Ephesus, will pass through Corinth on his way back to Ephesus. In his analysis of Timothy's travels, Trevijano writes:

> When Paul writes that letter [to the Corinthians] from Ephesus (1 Cor 16:8) Timothy is no longer with him (cf 1 Cor 1:1). Paul sent him to Corinth (1 Cor 4:17); nevertheless he foresaw that the letter would arrive before him (1 Cor 16:10-11). He must have sent it directly by ship, while Timothy went by land, making a trip through Macedonia and stopping over in Philippi. The trip of Timothy in Philippi, planned in Philippians 2:19, 23 would have been the same one mentioned here in 1 Cor 4:17; 16:10-11. Timothy left Ephesus for Corinth while passing through Philippi. Paul proposed to follow him later, both to Philippi (Phil 2:24) and on to Corinth (1 Cor 4:18-21). When he writes this first letter to the Corinthians, he counts on a sufficiently long interval before his trip in order to give time to Timothy to return (1 Cor 16:11). This is what was happening as he and his co-sender were writing 1 Cor 1:1. Paul's forthcoming trip is implicitly confirmed in what he says in 1 Cor 16:10-11. Consequently, the trip which Paul planned to take to Philippi (Phil 1:26; 2:24) has to be the one he intended to

take through Macedonia to Corinth (according to 2 Cor 2:13; 7:5).[4]

Trevijano situates the composition of Paul's letter to the Galatians before Paul left on this planned trip of his, and perhaps before the return of Timothy, who is not mentioned in the letter to the Galatians.

As the Pauline letters witness, Timothy was fundamental to Paul's information-exchange relation with the various Jesus groups that he had founded. Some would consider Timothy as Paul's envoy.[5] While "envoy" is a lovely image of Timothy's task, the problem is that Paul does not have sufficient political rank and appointment in the greater Greco-Roman world to be understood as capable of sending an envoy in the Roman Empire. Rather he is an apostle, a change agent, who like change agents the world over, has aides or assistants. These are coworkers, in Paul's terms. And Timothy was such a change-agent aide or coworker, presumably quite socially similar to the members of the Jesus groups that Paul had founded. Hence his success. And with the few lines at 1 Cor 16:10, Paul offers a sort of letter of recommendation for his coworker Timothy.

The Letter of Paul and Timothy to the Corinthians

Modern Pauline scholars consider the document called the second letter to the Corinthians to be a compilation of several letters written before and after an altercation between Paul and outsiders in that city.[6] The segments put together to form the present document are fragments of three letters plus other pieces. The topic of the letter is a dispute between the Pauline team and some interlopers. Letter 1 (2 Cor 2:14–6:13; 7:2-4) mirrors the situation before the dispute; letter 2 (2 Cor 10:1–13:14) was written during the dispute; and letter 3 (2 Cor 1:1–2:13; 7:5-16, in which Timothy figures) comes after the dispute. (Note that 8:1-24 is part of a letter of recommendation for Titus about the collection for Jerusalem; 9:1-15 is part of a letter about the collection for Jerusalem; and 6:14–7:1 is a non-Pauline fragment.) After Paul's dispute, at the time of the writing of this third letter, Timothy is again with Paul and cowrites the letter, which begins as expected:

> Paul, an apostle of Christ Jesus by the will of God, and Timothy our brother. To the church of God which is at Corinth, with all the saints who are in the whole of Achaia. (2 Cor 1:1)

Once again we have the usual Hellenistic opening, naming the sender, addressee, and greeting. Timothy, the letter's co-sender, is considered by Paul like a brother both in the Jesus group as well as in his change-agent activity. Obviously, as his co-sender, Paul believes that Timothy is genuinely concerned for the welfare of the Jesus groups Paul had founded. For this reason Timothy did more than simply transmit information from and to Paul. Such change-agent concern would be manifest in Timothy's change-agent tasks of diagnosing problems, solidifying the clients' intent to change, stabilizing the membership, and preventing discontinuance.

The letter is addressed not only to Jesus groups in Corinth but likewise to groups in Achaia. Achaia was the name of the Roman province in which Corinth was located. Notice that there is no usage of the word "Greece" to designate the territory of some collection of peoples called Greeks. (However, once in the New Testament, Acts 20:2, Achaia is referred to as "Greece."). "Greek" in Paul's time referred to the social status of people considered civilized, cultivated, well bred.

The Jesus groups founded by Paul consisted of Israelites designated Judeans and Greeks (1 Cor 1:24; Gal 3:28). Judeans were Israelites who adhered closely to the customs of Judea. Romans viewed the peoples of the Mediterranean as either barbarians or Greeks, and Judeans ranked among the barbarians. Hence Paul's description of his Jesus-group members as "Judeans and Greeks" meant uncultivated and civilized Israelites. These

are the weak and the strong one reads about in 1 Corinthians.
In Hellenistic society, the designation "weak" referred to persons
untrained in the customs and amenities of the cultivated strata
of society.[7] The "weak" Jesus-group members were the un-
Hellenized Israelites in the group.

To return to the so-called second letter to the Corinthians, the
opening chapter was written when Paul's conflict with his opponents was over. It presents a very incisive assessment of Paul's
coworkers. The passage runs:

> Because I was sure of this, I wanted to come to you first,
> so that you might have a double pleasure; I wanted to visit
> you on my way to Macedonia, and to come back to you
> from Macedonia and have you send me on my way to
> Judea. Was I vacillating when I wanted to do this? Do I make
> my plans like a worldly man, ready to say Yes and No at
> once? As surely as God is faithful, our word to you has not
> been Yes and No. For the Son of God, Jesus Christ, whom
> we preached among you, Silvanus and Timothy and I, was
> not Yes and No; but in him it is always Yes. For all the
> promises of God find their Yes in him. That is why we utter
> the Amen through him, to the glory of God. But it is God
> who establishes us with you in Christ, and has commis-
> sioned us; he has put his seal upon us and given us his
> Spirit in our hearts as a guarantee. (2 Cor 1:15-22)

In the course of reading the Pauline letters, one will find that
Paul and his coworkers were present-oriented persons. They
took their cues more often than not from revelations of God (that
is, altered states-of-consciousness experiences) rather than from
the forward planning we are used to. We find in these letters
that Paul often made travel plans (as here) but rarely seems to
have followed through with them (see 1 Thess 2:17-18; 1 Cor
4:18). He now states that he planned to go to Corinth in Achaia
on his way to Macedonia, then stop back in Corinth on his way
to Judea. Since Paul did not follow through with his travel plans,
he states two rhetorical questions that are meant to dodge accusations of hesitant uncertainty and inconsistency on his part.

Such accusations denigrate his honor. In a context marked by conflict with the Corinthians, aspersions on his honor may have been bruited around, given the fact that he never made the promised third visit to Corinth. Paul's inner circle of coworkers in Corinth would necessarily share in any dishonor affecting him personally. After all, he as well as his coworkers were collectivistic persons.

The phrase "As surely as God is faithful" is a word of honor, meant to demonstrate sincerity of intention and steadfastness of purpose. This word of honor functions like making an oath or swearing. To remove any shadow of ambiguity and untrustworthiness from himself and his aides, Paul adopts the procedure of identifying his team with their proclamation to the Corinthians. While Paul and Timothy collaborated on this letter, he lists his team here as "Silvanus and Timothy and I," the same trio that collaborated on the letter to the Thessalonians.

Paul's main point here: Given that the God of Israel raised Jesus from the dead, Jesus therefore is always an unambiguous and credible "Yes" to what these Israelite change agents have proclaimed in the name of the God of Israel. Their activity is rooted in God's promises, which are begun with Abraham and now in Christ and are unambiguously "Yes," so that we say "Amen," that is, we find them fully credible. And again Paul insists that it is God who founds these Jesus groups, the God of Israel who has established what would later be called "Christianity." As Paul insists, ". . . it is God who establishes us with you in Christ." He believes the God of Israel is the founder of these Jesus groups, and that it is the God of Israel who is the change agency for whom he and his aides work as a change-agent team. Further proof of this is the presence and activity of God's power, the Spirit of the God of Israel, who has marked Jesus-group change agents and group members, serving to guarantee their lifestyle in response to God's call.

In sum, there is no doubt that Timothy was a change agent who, like Silvanus, adopted the same perspective and insights about Jesus Christ, the Son of God, as did Paul. Paul trusted them and their way of proclaiming his gospel: that the God of

Israel raised Jesus from the dead, an event soon to be followed by the forthcoming kingdom of God. Timothy's understanding of the God of Israel and his revelation in Christ was just like Paul's. One might ask whether Paul's theology was Paul's alone or a theology developed with Timothy or with Timothy and Silvanus. Given the collectivist personality of these personages, the answer undoubtedly is "Yes." As with their collaborative letters, one cannot really mark off where one sender ends and the other begins.

The Letter of Paul and Timothy to the Philippians

The letter to the Philippians is another collaborative document that was the work of Paul and Timothy. Following the usual pattern of Hellenistic letters, this one begins as follows:

> Paul and Timothy, slaves of Christ Jesus, To all the saints in Christ Jesus who are at Philippi, with the bishops and deacons: (Phil 1:1)

Since the letter makes mention of Paul in prison (Phil 1:14), scholars concerned with calendric chronology generally locate the composition of this letter in either of the two places where Paul was known to have been in prison, namely, in Ephesus (rainy season AD 55–56) or in Rome (about AD 58–60).

In the superscription the co-senders interestingly designate themselves as "slaves" (NAB; RSV and NRSV have "servants"). They are metaphorical "slaves of Christ Jesus." Slaves were not simply servants; they were persons socially situated in the social institution called "slavery." Slavery began with a symbolic ritual of dishonor (social death—self- or other-inflicted) that resulted in depriving a person of freedom of decision and action by means of force or enforced solidarity with a view to the social utility of the enslaving agent. Slavery was a subset-set of kinship (domestic slavery) or of politics (political slavery: temple slaves, city slaves, and the like). The main result of being enslaved was that slaves were totally deprived of freedom of decision and action on their own behalf. To be slaves of Jesus Christ meant that Paul and Timothy were for the utility of Jesus Christ, who controlled their choices and actions by their becoming part and parcel of their owner, a social relation of embeddedness in or solidarity with their owner, Christ Jesus. While their description of themselves as metaphorical slaves of Christ might sound odd to us, the fact is that the metaphor made total sense in a society where such slaves might be met throughout any city.

Equally interesting is the fact that the co-senders make no mention of a "church" at Philippi; instead, they designate Philippian Jesus-group members as "saints." This word indicates emphasis on the status of the Philippians before God and toward one another rather than on their being constituted by God into a community. "Saints" is not a moral designation as it is for us. For example, in English a saint is a morally good and holy person, and a saintly deed is a positive moral action. The moral overtones of the term derive from later centuries. In first-century Israel the term "saint" (and its synonyms "holy ones," "sacred ones") refers to people set apart by and for God, people exclusively God's (see 2 Cor 1:1; 9:1; 13:12; also 1 Thess 3:13; 1 Cor 1:2; 6:2; 16:1, 15; Rom 1:7). The word emphasizes exclusivity, hence a bounded, centripetal ingroup.

"In Christ Jesus" describes how these saints are set off from other groups. Their group is in Christ Jesus instead of in Israel (that is, in Jacob) or any other founding personage. The focus here is on the horizontal—on the ingroup and on the significance of membership in a Jesus group. All members are in Christ and constitute (the body of) Christ.

With the greeting, the senders fall back on stereotypical usage (Gal 1:3; 1 Cor 1:3; 2 Cor 1:2; Rom 1:7; Phlm 1). The wish for the favor (grace) of the gods or of God, along with peace, is very common in Hellenistic letters. The special feature in Pauline letters is the assignment of this grace and peace as coming from God our Father and the Lord Jesus Christ. God, of course, is the God of Israel, the Jesus-group patron who provides favor (grace);

Jesus Christ in turn is Lord, the person raised by God, now with authority and dominion.

In context, the greeting has a vertical dimension. As always, "from God the Father" indicates Paul's perspective as essentially theologically motivated, that is, God-initiated, with the God of Israel as the main actor in Jesus-group formation, support, and activity. It might be important to repeat that when our senders use the word "God," they mean the God of Israel. After all, as previously noted, they live and work in a world where there are "many 'gods' and many 'lords'—yet for us there is one God, the Father, from whom are all things and for whom we exist, and one Lord, Jesus Christ, through whom are all things and through whom we exist" (1 Cor 8:5-6). Paul, Timothy, and their Jesus groups call the God of Israel "Father," a word deriving from the kinship institution and often used as a rather formal title in the kin-like relationship of social superior to inferior called patronage. In Aramaic this designation is "Abba," meaning "O Father." The word does not mean "Daddy," as it does in the recent language called modern Israeli Hebrew. For Paul and Timothy, the God of Israel is most often described as "Father" or patron of the gathering summoned by God. For the significance of the role of "the Lord Jesus Christ," re-read the previous explanation of the superscription of 1 Thessalonians above (pp. 75–76).

The Greek word translated "bishop" (1:1) is *episkopos*, a word that literally means "supervisor," "supervising manager." This is the first time that the word appears in the New Testament. Since the Pauline Jesus groups looked forward to the forthcoming kingdom of God, the interim supervisory or managerial role in these fictive kin groups was not yet as formally organized. It is important not to retroject modern meanings into the New Testament. These bishops at Philippi were nothing like contemporary bishops in churches that resulted from the separation of church and state in the eighteenth century. From the period of Emperor Constantine (AD 306–337) until the eighteenth century, bishops held a political office, part of the political-religious institution, salaried by the government and with political authority in their domain. In the first century these supervisors had no legal or formal authority, since people could enter and leave Jesus groups at will. These groups were elective associations. On the other hand, the supervisors did attend to the welfare of the group consisting of collectivistic persons in a collectivistic ingroup. Two generations after Paul and Timothy, the social role of Jesus-group supervisor would become somewhat institutionalized as fictive kin-group manager, that is, as officer in an elective association. We will consider this point as evidenced in the third Pauline-generation documents called the letters to Timothy and Titus.

The word "deacon" here is a transliteration of the Greek *diakonos*. In the Hellenistic world the word normally referred to someone functioning as an agent of a higher-ranking person, either as an intermediary in commercial transactions or as a messenger or diplomat. Perhaps these deacons were persons in the service of the supervising manager or of the Jesus group in general.

Paul is ever concerned with maintaining an information-exchange relationship with all the Jesus groups that he had helped to establish. And while he has this letter sent off to the Philippians, he would like to hear from them soon. He states:

> I hope in the Lord Jesus to send Timothy to you soon, so that I may be cheered by news of you. (Phil 2:19)

Once more Timothy is to travel on behalf of the Pauline team, in which Paul himself is much invested (previously, see 1 Thess 3:2, 6; 1 Cor 4:17). In this way Timothy carried out a task essential to Paul's change-agent task. And again Paul expresses the quality of his relationship with Timothy, like father to son (Phil 2:22), a very close relationship indeed. As an aside, Paul tells of some Jesus-group change agents who seek their own interests and not those of Jesus Christ. What these interests might be, Paul does not say, in his usual, high-context way. More importantly, Paul believes that Timothy is genuinely concerned for the welfare of the Philippians; hence he does more than transmit information. Rather, his concern would be to support the interpersonal relationship growing among Jesus-group members and his team as well as to carry out his change-agent tasks of diagnosing problems, solidifying the clients' intent to change, stabilizing the membership, and preventing discontinuance. The Philippians know Timothy and his follow-up change-agent activity in the work of the gospel of God. So Paul hopes to send him and to follow after him soon (Phil 2:23-24).

The Letter of Paul and Timothy to Philemon

The final collaborative letter of Paul and Timothy is the brief letter to a certain Philemon. In the superscription the document reads:

> Paul, a prisoner for Christ Jesus, and Timothy our brother,
> To Philemon our beloved fellow worker. (Phlm 1)

Among the notable features of this letter, the first is that while a number of persons are mentioned at the end of the letter as sending greetings to Philemon, Timothy does not rank among them but is situated in fact as co-sender of the letter. This indicates his hands-on function in having collaborated in formulating this letter. Another point is that only Paul presents himself as "prisoner of Christ Jesus," while Timothy is free. While the letter later explains that Paul is being held as a prisoner, this superscription underscores the fact that the one who really holds Paul as prisoner is Jesus Christ. The superscription further notes that Philemon is beloved person and coworker of both Paul and Timothy. Like Timothy, Philemon too is a "brother," that is, fellow Jesus-group member. The kinship terminology points to Jesus groups as fictive kin groups.

But more than this, Paul and Timothy call Philemon their "beloved fellow worker." The NRSV translates "beloved" (Greek: *agapētos*) as "friend." "Friend" is often a technical term in Hellenistic Greek, designating one who is a client of some patron. Paul does not use that term here; rather, he calls Philemon "beloved" a term that further underscores a fellow ingroup member, bound by loyalty and solidarity. In the Mediterranean world, past and present, the word "beloved" is used by both genders of both genders. Paul also calls him "fellow worker," a term he seems to use for first adopters of the innovation he communicated with his gospel of God.

Cross-cultural studies of first adopters indicate that as a rule they control adequate material and personality resources to absorb the possible failure should the innovation prove unsuccessful.[8] The fact that Philemon owns a house, and that he owns a slave such as Onesimus, as we learn later in the letter, indicates that he does have adequate material resources. The usual qualities of first adopters include the ability to understand and apply rather complex knowledge; venturesomenesss, that is, a willingness to undertake the hazardous, the rash, the daring, the risky; and finally, cosmopoliteness, that is, having contact with outsiders, with more cosmopolite social relationships. Should one try to imagine Philemon's personal resources, such stereotypical traits would be of utility. And we might recall here that a Hellenistic Israelite such as Timothy was also a first adopter.

The Letter of Paul to the Romans

Timothy is mentioned in the last chapter of the letter to the Romans. Romans, like Galatians, was sent by Paul alone. However, the last chapter of Romans (Rom 16) has the form of a letter of recommendation for a significant person in Paul's Jesus groups named Phoebe. Many scholars believe that this last chapter was appended to the letter to the Romans. Originally it was a letter to the Jesus group(s) at Ephesus and was composed by Paul on Phoebe's behalf. Such letters of recommendation were well known in antiquity, and the practice of writing such letters was adopted by Jesus groups as well. As previously noted, 2 Corinthians 8 was such a letter of recommendation, sent by Paul and Timothy on behalf of Titus.

At the close of this letter, Paul notes to the Ephesians:

> Timothy, my fellow worker, greets you; so do Lucius and
> Jason and Sosipater, my kinsmen. (Rom 16:21)

What we learn from this note is what has been apparent all
along, namely, that Timothy was Paul's coworker in the task of
proclaiming the gospel of God revealed to Paul. This greeting
presupposes that Timothy is known to the Ephesians, to whom
he sends regards.

Conclusion

From these cursory considerations of the authentic letters of
Paul and Timothy, we learn several significant pieces of information about Timothy.

First of all, Timothy was committed to the God of Israel as
that God revealed himself in his raising Jesus from the dead. He
believed Paul's conclusion that this meant that the God of Israel
would soon inaugurate a theocracy, the kingdom of heaven,
marked by the return of Jesus as Messiah and Lord. In these
high-context writings, it is presumed that all Israelites knew that
this coming of Jesus would take place over Jerusalem, since it
was through the opening in the sky over Jerusalem that Jesus
was taken up by God (Luke 24:51; Acts 1:9; Stephen looks
through this opening in the sky to see Jesus with God in Acts
7:56). As he went, so he would return. When Jesus returned, all
those Israelites who believe in what their God had done would
be taken up toward Jerusalem, whether living or dead, to take
part in this new theocracy.

Second, we learn that Timothy belonged to the status of the
"Greeks." He was civilized by Mediterranean standards, since
he could readily travel to the significant Hellenistic cities of the
Roman Empire and deal with resident Hellenistic Israelites on
their terms. His successful trips to Philippi, Thessalonika, and

Corinth as change-agent aide shows his social abilities in this regard. He was homophilous with the Hellenistic Israelites, meaning that he shared the customs, language, and style of Hellenistic Israelites in a non-Israelite majority city. His successful mediations indicate that perhaps he was more at home in those social settings (more homophilous) than Paul.

Third, we likewise learn that Timothy was known to Jesus groups around the Adriatic—in Thessalonika, Philippi, Corinth, as well as Ephesus.

These letters give no indication of Timothy's place of origin. For that matter, they say nothing about Paul's place of origin either. Given the expert use of Israel's sacred writings in these letters, it is obvious that Paul and Timothy both (or singly) knew these writings in Greek. Given the fact that Paul states that he was of the Pharisees and persecuted Jesus-group members in Judea, one would think that it was Timothy who was at home in the Septuagint, the Greek version of Israel's sacred writings.

In sum, the evidence concerning Timothy's contribution to the proclamation of the gospel and the formation and support of Jesus groups is significant. Given our hindsight, it seems doubtful whether Paul's successes in his change-agent tasks would have been realized without the able assistance of Timothy, his collaborator and co-composer of his letters. This judgment is further corroborated by the fact that even in the next two Pauline generations, Timothy continues to stand out quite prominently in the memory of those first-century Jesus-group members.

CHAPTER 5

The Timothy Tradition Begins: Third-Generation Recollections

I n the previous chapter we considered authentic, first-generation information about Timothy. We found that he was a significant co-sender of several significant Pauline letters. Further, those documents attest to a person much appreciated and praised as coworker by that master Jesus-group change agent, Paul. In this chapter we consider how Timothy was remembered by third Pauline-generation persons, persons who were very proud of what Paul, Silvanus, Timothy, and their colleagues had accomplished. After all, these men were their ancestors in faith. While some would recall what Paul and his team accomplished in terms of traditions about the gospel of God that they received, others wished to know the story of these men, what they actually did.

As noted previously, the two volumes called the Gospel of Luke and the Acts of the Apostles are in fact the work of an anonymous writer (as are all the gospels). This two-volume work traces back to the fourth generation in the Jesus tradition and has been conveniently labeled the work of one "Luke." Given the writer's extensive interest in the story of Paul and given the principle of third-generation interest (see chap. 2), it seems that

Luke belonged to the third Pauline generation, a generation that reflected upon the origins of its Jesus-group's founder(s).

Luke tells the story of Paul as remembered in his generation and locale. In the process he emphasizes a number of things. He describes Paul largely as a prophet with a message from the God of Israel to be made known to the people of Israel. However, unlike the Twelve, whose activity is largely confined to Judea and immediate vicinity, Paul's commission embraces Israelite communities located in majority non-Israelite cities in the northeast region of the Mediterranean. The focal persons in the book of Acts are Peter in the first part and Paul in the second.

There is much discussion among modern scholars concerning Luke's sources for what he says about these men. Unlike his story of Jesus, based upon narratives composed in the generation before his, Luke's story of the Jerusalemite Jesus group and of Paul's change-agent travels does not seem to be based on previous narratives. Yet it would be an error in method to expect a first-century writer to follow the canons of post-Enlightenment historiography. Luke was a first-century, high-context writer. He prefaces his volumes with a prologue in the fashion of first- and second-century historians. He undoubtedly told his readers in an orderly way everything they needed to know to understand their origins and the activities of their ancestors in faith. Here, of course, we focus on what Luke tells about Timothy.

Paul and Barnabas: How Paul Chose Timothy

Luke introduces Timothy into his story of Paul in the passage labeled Acts 15:35–16:13 as follows:

> But Paul and Barnabas remained in Antioch, teaching and preaching the word of the Lord, with many others also.
>
> And after some days Paul said to Barnabas, "Come, let us return and visit the brethren in every city where we proclaimed the word of the Lord, and see how they are." And Barnabas wanted to take with them John called Mark.

But Paul thought best not to take with them one who had withdrawn from them in Pamphylia, and had not gone with them to the work. And there arose a sharp contention, so that they separated from each other; Barnabas took Mark with him and sailed away to Cyprus, but Paul chose Silas and departed, being commended by the brethren to the grace of the Lord. And he went through Syria and Cilicia, strengthening the churches.

And he came also to Derbe and to Lystra. A disciple was there, named Timothy, the son of a Jewish woman who was a believer; but his father was a Greek. He was well spoken of by the brethren at Lystra and Iconium. Paul wanted Timothy to accompany him; and he took him and circumcised him because of the Jews that were in those places, for they all knew that his father was a Greek. As they went on their way through the cities, they delivered to them for observance the decisions which had been reached by the apostles and elders who were at Jerusalem. So the churches were strengthened in the faith, and they increased in numbers daily.

And they went through the region of Phrygia and Galatia, having been forbidden by the Holy Spirit to speak the word in Asia. And when they had come opposite Mysia, they attempted to go into Bithynia, but the Spirit of Jesus did not allow them; so, passing by Mysia, they went down to Troas. And a vision appeared to Paul in the night: a man of Macedonia was standing beseeching him and saying, "Come over to Macedonia and help us." And when he had seen the vision, immediately we sought to go on into Macedonia, concluding that God had called us to preach the gospel to them.

Setting sail therefore from Troas, we made a direct voyage to Samothrace, and the following day to Neapolis, and from there to Philippi, which is the leading city of the district of Macedonia, and a Roman colony. We remained in this city some days; and on the sabbath day we went outside the gate to the riverside, where we supposed there was a place of prayer; and we sat down and spoke to the women who had come together. (Acts 15:35–16:13)

It is useful to follow Luke's story with a map. At times one can readily correlate Luke's story with what Paul states or hints at in his letters, and at other times the account of Acts is otherwise unverifiable. Interestingly, the writer of Acts never mentions that Paul and his co-senders ever wrote any letters at all. But in the process of telling a coherent third-generation story, Luke follows his own sources of information for the most part. His main third- generation goal is to tell the life of Paul and fill in what is necessary in order to understand what God did in the career and activity of Paul. What counts is to tell the story of Paul in some valid and adequate way. In this story one finds that a very significant person in Luke's third-generation Jesus groups is Barnabas, a close associate of Paul's (or vice-versa initially). The passage introducing Timothy and cited above presumes that one knows about the relationship of Barnabas and Paul and how they split up. It was this split that occasioned Paul's inviting Timothy to join him.

Why Paul Chose Timothy

In the account of Acts, Barnabas emerges as a very important person in Paul's story. His full name was Joseph Barnabas, a Levite and native of the island of Cyprus (Acts 4:36). He was responsible for introducing Saul (Paul) to the circle of the first-generation apostles in Jerusalem (Acts 9:27). Paul recalls this event in his letter to the Galatians (2:1-14). After this episode the writer of Acts notes that Barnabas had to fetch Paul from Tarsus to assist him in his work of proclamation and teaching in Antioch (Acts 11:25; there were two cities named Antioch, one in Pisidia, now central Turkey, and the other in Syria; Antioch here is the one in Syria, which had a sizable Israelite population). Later the two bring famine relief to Jesus-group elders in Jerusalem (Acts 11:30).

Following an altered state-of-consciousness experience of the Spirit, Jesus-group prophets in Antioch sent Barnabas and Saul off on a task determined by God (Acts 13:1-2), to proclaim the word of God to Israelites in Cyprus, and from there to Perga, and finally to Antioch in Pisidia (Acts 13:13-16). After Saul's synagogue proclamation there, Luke now switches to a Hellenistic name and refers to this change agent as Paul. He keeps that designation up to the end of the work. Likewise, it was at Antioch in Pisidia that Paul and Barnabas proclaimed the word to non-Israelites (Acts 13:48-51) before being driven out by local Judeans and moving on to Iconium (Acts 13:51). Barnabas and Paul work as a team in Iconium, then move on to Derbe after an attempt was made on Paul's life by Judeans (Acts 14:1-20). From Derbe they went on to Lystra, then on to Iconium and Antioch, Perga and Attalia, and back to Antioch in Syria (Acts 14:21-28).

The purpose for this long digression is to show that Barnabas and Paul were coworking change agents for some time and in a good number of cities. They had success with non-Israelites, although no specific non-Israelites are mentioned, and the story does not suggest how these non-Israelites fit into the local Jesus groups. To explain this, Luke provides a passage from Isaiah 49:6 that echoes Luke 2:32: "I will give you as a light to the nations, that my salvation may reach to the end of the earth." The passage from Isaiah is ambiguous in that Israel was meant to be a light among non-Israelites, with salvation reaching all Israelites (to the end of the earth). Luke applies the idea as salvation to non-Israelites themselves, again without specifying in what that salvation might consist. The story of God's initiative relative to Cornelius's and Peter's follow-up provides some suggestion, with non-Israelites fully subordinate to Israelite Jesus-group members (see Acts 10).

Now, thanks to Barnabas and Paul and their successes among non-Israelites, the apostles and elders of the Jerusalem Jesus group agree that non-Israelites in Israelite Jesus groups would not have to be circumcised or keep to kosher rules in foods and calendar. Their only obligation was to follow the four prohibitions listed in the Torah (in the book of Leviticus) that obliged non-Israelites resident among Israelites in Judea (see Lev 17:8, 10, 13; 20:2; and Acts 15:23-29: they had to "abstain from what has been sacrificed to idols and from blood and from what is strangled and from unchastity"—v. 29). In other words, given the Israelite majority in Jesus groups, non-Israelites belonged as resident aliens. According to Acts, Paul and Barnabas then carried this decree to Antioch (Acts 15:30).

To return to the episode in Acts cited above (Acts 15:35–16:13), Acts 15:39 is the last mention of Barnabas in the story. After that point the writer shifts full focus on Paul and his team of coworkers. And in this passage we learn much about Paul. First we find him in Antioch with Barnabas, his senior in the Jesus group and fellow change agent, "with many others." Antioch seems to have had a large Israelite community, with well-established Jesus groups. The people mentioned here all have Semitic names, apart from Paul, whose name was previously changed in the story from the Semitic Saul to the Hellenistic Paul. Barnabas, John, and Silas are all Semitic names; they are "Judeans."

The episode opens with Paul, as good change agent, suggesting it is time to visit the Jesus groups previously founded, a part of the process of maintaining an information-exchange relation and stabilizing and preventing discontinuance of the innovation presented there. Barnabas agreed with the idea but wanted to take along another change-agent aide, John Mark. Paul was against taking him, since, as Luke previously reported, John Mark had once abandoned them (Acts 13:13 and here). Paul's decision seems to have been an affront to Barnabas's honor, since Barnabas chose to take John Mark along. The result was a "sharp contention" between the two (v. 39). So Barnabas and John Mark left by sea for Cyprus, from where Barnabas came. Paul and Silas went by land to Derbe and then Lystra, where they meet up with one Timothy.

Timothy's Background

As a good third Pauline-generation writer, Luke provides further information about Timothy. First we learn that Timothy lived in Lystra when Paul recruited him. Lystra was a Roman colony (as were Pisidian Antioch [Acts 13:14], Troas [16:8], Corinth [18:1], and Philippi [16:12]). Luke says nothing about where Timothy might have been born. However, he does specify that Timothy was the son of a Judean woman and a Greek father and that he had a fine reputation among Jesus-group members in nearby towns. Most commentators presume that Timothy's father, being a Greek, was therefore a non-Israelite; however, the word "Greek" referred to a social status. And in Israelite ingroups, "Judean" meant "barbarian," that is, following the customs and language of Judea, while "Greek" meant "civilized," following Hellenistic customs and language. Timothy did issue from a mixed marriage but from one of mixed cultures. His name is Greek, and as we learn later, he was not subject to the Judean barbaric custom of genital mutilation called circumcision (Acts 16:3).

The Judean-Greek terminology may be confusing, so consider the following chart.

From an Israelite perspective when speaking in Judea, Galilee, or Perea		
With ingroup persons	Individually: Judeans Galileans Pereans	Collectively: House of Israel
With outgroup persons	Individually: Romans Corinthians Philippians, etc.	Collectively: The people (other than Israel), Gentiles

From an Israelite perspective when speaking outside Judea, Galilee, or Perea		
Speaking with fellow Israelites:	About the ingroup: general name is Israel, broken down into Judeans (barbarians) and Greeks (Hellenes) or Territory names	About the outgroup: general name is Gentiles or the people (other than Israel), non-Israelite
Speaking with non-Israelites: (Gentiles)	About the ingroup: Judeans	About the outgroup: specific non-Israelite group names: Romans, Corinthians, etc.

This sort of language designation, based on mental boundary shifting, should not be difficult to understand. For example, when two U.S. persons in the U.S. ask each other, "What is your nationality?" they invariably means "What is the country of origin of your ancestors who came to the U.S." But should two U.S. persons in London be asked by a Londoner, "What is your nationality?" both would quickly answer "American." The change in response points to a change in perception of ingroup (we) and outgroup (they) boundaries. So too in antiquity. Among Israelites in Palestine, there were only Judeans from Judea, Galileans from Galilee, and Pereans from Perea; all three together formed the house of Israel. However, among non-Israelites in Palestine and anyplace else, all members of the house of Israel were "Judeans." But among Israelites in majority non-Israelite cities, fellow Israelites were either "Judeans" (unacquainted with Hellenistic customs and language) or "Greeks" (civilized and educated in Hellenistic customs).

What is important to note is that in this usage, the opposite of Judean is never Gentile (meaning non-Israelite). The opposite of Gentile or non-Israelite is Israelite. That modern Bible readers speak of "Jews and Gentiles" indicates how far they have departed from first-century biblical usage. These terms never stand together in the New Testament (the sole and closest instance is Galatians 2:14-15, contrasting Judean customs with the non-Israelite). Hence to bring this modern companion pair of words to New Testament reading has led and will continue to lead to great confusion.

To return to the story in Acts, Luke next tells us that "Paul wanted Timothy to accompany him; and he took him and circumcised him because of the Jews that were in those places, for they all knew that his father was a Greek" (16:3). And right after that they traveled on. One might wonder what sort of circumcision enables an adult male to take up traveling by foot so quickly after such a sensitive operation. This sequence of circumcision and quick traveling should give one pause. What exactly was this circumcision?

Many think that in antiquity the main infallible and usable marker distinguishing an Israelite from a non-Israelite was a form of male genital mutilation called circumcision, the removal of the foreskin. The reason for this is that many believe that the story of Israel-in-the-Bible is the actual story of a historical entity called Israel. However, the historical fact is that in the period of the Persian empire (fifth century BC), what was left of historical Israel was Samaria. The new Persian colony of Yahud, founded thanks to the "Donation of Cyrus" (2 Chr 36:22-23) by a handful of returning Persian transferred elites, required a foundation story (often called "the return from the Exile") as well as a set of stories to enable the rather small Persian colonial enclave to establish the antiquity of these immigrants in the Persian colony of Yahud (later Judea). This set of stories, composed by elite scribes, resulted in the biblical story of Israel-in-the-Bible (to be distinguished from historical Israel, that is, Samaria). This account, mixing myth and legend, provided credentials for these new Judeans to claim to be "true Israel."

> [By] the third century BC, Judea proper was a small part of Palestine: it was almost identifiable with the territory of the city of Jerusalem, and as such it was still envisaged by Polybius in the middle of the second century BC (16, fr. 39). Samaria and Galilee were outside it. The Samaritans—or at least those of them who were not entirely Hellenized— had built up a religious center of their own on Mount Gerizim in circumstances which contradictory legends had rendered unrecognizable. A council of laymen and priests under the presidency of the High Priest had a large measure of autonomy in its government of Jerusalem, but the presence of Ptolemaic garrison in the country must be assumed.[1]

The point of this historical excursion is that the Old Testament law about infant male genital mutilation, done on the eighth day after birth (Lev 12:3, a practice retrojected into the story of Gen 17:10-14), is a legend collated by Persian-period Judean scribes.

Shaye Cohen, an American Jewish scholar, has demonstrated that circumcision as an Israelite marker was rather late in Judea, evidenced only during the Maccabean period, about 150 BC. It took several centuries before the new Judean practice reached Israelite colonies far from Judea. And, of course, most Israelites residing among non-Israelite Hellenistic populations would consider the practice barbaric mutilation and would not adopt it. What this means is that "Greek" Israelite parents, such as Timothy's father, would surely not allow his son to be mutilated in this totally un-Greek (that is, uncivilized) way.

Furthermore, the symbolic genital mutilation practiced at this time was certainly not the removal of the foreskin. There are two good reasons for this position. The first reason is that Israelites could have their circumcision normalized. Paul mentions "removing the marks of circumcision" in 1 Cor 7:18. Hellenizing Judeans

> tried to hide their circumcision through *epispasm*, the "stretching" or "drawing down" of the remains of the foreskin so that the penis would have the look of an uncircumcised organ. Those who joined the Maccabean state were circumcised as well. Greek historians recounting the Maccabean conquests knew the importance of circumcision to the Maccabees, but over a century had to elapse before outsiders began to associate circumcision with Judaism in the diaspora. The association is documented by one Latin writer in Rome in the second half of the first century BC (Horace) and by a string of Latin writers from the middle of the first century AD to the first quarter of the second century AD (Persius, Petronius, Martial, Suetonius, Tacitus, Juvenal)[2]

The point Cohen makes here is that the innovation of circumcision practiced in Palestine from about 150 BC was not identical with circumcision as practiced by Talmudic rabbinism and its recent Jewishness. The reason for this is that the practice of epispasm allowed for the undoing of the mutilation of circumcision.

Moreover, one cannot presume non-Israelite identity by reference to lack of circumcision. Many members of the much older house of Israel (Samaria) were spread around the Mediterranean long before the Maccabean political reforms of 150 BC. With the slow rate of information flow in antiquity, as well as the high degree of assimilation and accommodation of Israelites in various communities outside of Palestine, many of these Israelites were little concerned with the new trends and customs begun in upstart, "barbarian" Judea.

A second good reason for doubting that "circumcision" at the time of Paul and Timothy entailed the removal of the foreskin is the fact that it was only sometime after the Bar-Kochba incident in Judea, that is, about AD 150, that ben Zakkaist groups of Pharisaic scribes (later called rabbis) introduced the requirement of the removal of the whole foreskin (Hebrew: *peri'ah*). With the whole foreskin removed, *epispasmos*, or the restoration of what remained of the foreskin and sewing it in place, would be prevented; there would be nothing left to restore.[3] At least among ben Zakkaist rabbis (Pharisees), the removal of the whole foreskin was a post-mid-second century AD requirement, hence well after the time of Paul and Timothy.

Since Paul's circumcising Timothy did not entail the "surgical" removal of the entire foreskin, that would explain how Paul might make a small cut in the foreskin to draw blood (a basic requirement in "circumcision"), and shortly after Timothy could travel with him. As Luke explains in the story, Paul "circumcised" Timothy so that he might be acceptable to interact with Judeans. In the Acts story, Paul, Silas (Silvanus in Greek), and Timothy had as their task to deliver the decisions of the Jerusalemite apostles and elders (Acts 15:28-29) relative to requirements for non-Israelites who were resident aliens. There is no such information about some "Jerusalemite apostolic decree" in any of the authentic Pauline letters. Hence it is likely that this is a third Pauline-generation scenario of how things went in the past, since it mirrored the practice among these third generation-Pauline Jesus groups of Luke's day.

Timothy's Travels

Next Luke describes the itinerary followed by Paul, Silas, and Timothy, an itinerary in fact drawn up by the Holy Spirit (again, in an altered state-of-consciousness experience): through Phrygia and Galatia but not Asia, to the region of Mysia but not to Mysia and not to Bithynia, and eventually to Troas (Acts 16:6-8). And finally and more specifically, Paul has a vision of a Macedonian inviting him to that region. What is going on here? As frequently in Acts, a number of Jesus-group members have altered states-of-consciousness experiences attributed to God's Spirit (see chap. 3, pp. 50ff., about altered states of consciousness).

Following these divine directives, the three set sail from the Roman colony of Troas to Neapolis, the seaport town on the road to "Philippi, which is the leading city of the district of Macedonia, and a Roman colony" (Acts 16:12). On the sabbath they seek out an Israelite gathering or synagogue, which they found at the riverside of the city. Interestingly, they find a gathering of Israelite women, and to them they proclaim the gospel of the God of Israel. The following episode concerning Lydia of Thyatira and her household (Acts 16:14-15) opens a series of incidents that involve Paul and Silas. Timothy falls by the way. Scholars find it surprising that he is not mentioned in the accounts of quite notable events, first in Philippi (imprisonment in Acts 16:16-40), and then in Thessalonika (riot in Acts 17:1-9). Luke does not explain this omission.

On the other hand, after the riot in Thessalonika, the Jesus-group members in that city spirit Paul and Silas off to Beroea, "and when they arrived they went into the Judean synagogue" (Acts 17:10). Of course, a Judean synagogue would be the opposite of a Greek synagogue—both groups being Israelite. We find a similar reference in verse 12, speaking of many Judeans believing Paul's explained gospel, as well as high-standing Greek women and Greek men. The Thessalonian Judeans were still aggrieved by Paul's actions of splitting the synagogue membership with his proclamation of the gospel of God. When they came down to Beroea, the local Jesus-group members accompanied Paul by sea to Athens, while Silas and Timothy remained there, although they later received a command to come to Paul as soon as possible (Acts 17:15). Presumably the two then followed on to Athens. Once more, however, nothing is said about their activity.

Luke picks up on Silas and Timothy after Paul leaves Athens and gets to Corinth (Acts 18:1). In this description the two never really left Macedonia but simply moved on to Corinth to be with Paul: "When Silas and Timothy arrived from Macedonia, Paul was occupied with preaching, testifying to the Judeans that the Christ was Jesus" (Acts 18:5; RSV reads "Jews" instead of "Judeans"). Again nothing is said about what these two were doing, although Paul stayed in Corinth for a year and a half, "teaching the word of God among them" (Acts 18:11).

In the next episode involving Timothy, we learn that he is with Paul in Ephesus, where Paul did extraordinary feats. Once more Paul has an instructing altered state-of-consciouness experience: "After these events Paul resolved in the Spirit to pass through Macedonia and Achaia and go to Jerusalem, saying, 'After I have been there, I must also see Rome'" (19:21). Paul then sends Timothy and Erastus into Macedonia, while he stays on in Ephesus, only to experience another riot, after which he moves on to Macedonia (Acts 19:22–20:1).

The last mention of Timothy occurs as Paul decides to leave by boat for Syria. Once more his aggrieved Judean opposition sought to do him in, so instead of sailing, he went by the land route through Macedonia, presumably to Philippi and on to Troas, with an entourage of seven Jesus-group members, among whom was Timothy (Acts 20:2-4). At Troas the group stayed for seven days, with Paul intending to go on.

So ends Luke's recollection of Timothy. While it is not as much as one might like, it is significant in that Luke assumes that Timothy was an Israelite in a predominantly non-Israelite region, a perfect homophilous candidate to assist Paul in his diffusion of innovation activity among Israelites in majority non-Israelite locations. Recall that "homophilous" means sharing a rather large number of social characteristics in common, such as language, customs, shared history and outlook, and the like. Timothy was raised as a "civilized" person; his father was Greek, and he bore a Greek name; hence he knew his way among civilized Israelite circles of the northeastern Mediterranean. And after Paul recruited him, he traveled extensively in the service of the gospel of the God of Israel, to inform fellow Israelites of Jesus' resurrection and appointment by God as Israel's Messiah who would usher in a forthcoming theocracy in Jerusalem. All these high-context items are packed into the Luke's third-generation story of Paul and his significant coworker Timothy.

Luke never mentions the letter-writing activity of Paul, Silas, and Timothy. In his view, the information-exchange relation expected of change agents was always carried on in interpersonal, face-to-face ways, either by Paul himself or his chosen aides, such as Timothy. Interestingly, Luke never mentions Titus, even though third-generation Jesus-group members did hold him in great respect, as we know from the so-called letter of Paul to Titus. Perhaps he omits mention of Titus because Titus, working on Paul's behalf, dealt with rather stormy situations in his attempt to stabilize some of Paul's Jesus groups and to prevent discontinuance of the innovation proclaimed by Paul (2 Cor 2:13; 7:6, 13; 8:6, 16, 23; 12:18; Gal 2:1, 3).

Conclusion

In describing the mention of Timothy in the third Pauline-generation memory of the writer of the Acts of the Apostles, we learn some details of Timothy's life. Given the principle of third-generation interest, this is something one might expect of one telling the story of Paul, since as we learned from the Pauline letters, Timothy was a significant coworker in the proclamation of the gospel of God. In Luke-Acts, we learn of the origins of Timothy, a Hellenistic Israelite from Lystra. We find out why

Paul chose Timothy and requested his assistance in face of his split with Barnabas over John Mark. This split is what occasioned Timothy's entering the story of Paul. We are told that Timothy's mother was Judean and his father Greek. His father's civilized background explains why Timothy might be an "uncircumcised" Israelite. And Paul's plan for him explains why Timothy underwent that Torah ritual in spite of the decree of the Jerusalem Council, which he was to make known to non-Israelites in Jesus groups. Finally, Luke offers a sketch of Timothy's travels on behalf of the gospel of God, although no mention is made of any specific dimensions of these travels. For information in this regard, the Pauline letters are indispensable.

In sum, from Luke-Acts we learn who Timothy was, where he was from, and under what circumstances he joined up with Paul. These third Pauline-generation recollections of the life of this ancestor in faith better situates the person named Timothy in the authentic Pauline letters. They provide a rather full first-century description of a human being in terms of the criteria of gender, genealogy, and geography.[4]

CHAPTER 6

The Second Letter of Paul and Timothy to the Thessalonians: About Forgery

To assist in the process of locating New Testament documents in some time sequence, in chapter 3 we discussed the principle of third-generation interest. To recall, the principle states that when a first generation has experienced significant and irreversible change rooted in some appreciable social alteration, in response to this experienced change the second generation seeks to ignore (hence "forget") many dimensions of first-generation experience, while the third generation seeks to remember and recover what the second generation sought to forget. We believe that this principle applied to the Jesus groups founded by Paul. The second generation after Paul was undoubtedly struck by Paul's death, given his view that he would be around to experience the transformation to be wrought by the coming kingdom of God (see 1 Cor 15:51: "we shall all not sleep . . .," that is, die).

There does not seem to be much left from the generation after Paul, the second Pauline generation. However, there is one document among the Pauline letters that ignores or forgets much of what we know as first-generation Pauline expectations. That document is the second letter to the Thessalonians. Pauline scholars consider this letter as post-Pauline, yet they generally overlook the significance of collaboration, and this letter, like the first letter to the Thessalonians, is presented as a letter of Paul, Silvanus, and Timothy.

The appreciable social change that faced the second Pauline generation was the unexpected death of Paul without the coming of the kingdom in Jerusalem. To call this a "delay of the parousia" or a "delay of the coming of the kingdom" is undoubtedly what such an experience would mean to us with our post-Enlightenment sense of time and calendar. However, in the ancient Mediterranean, focused on the present, "on time" always referred to when the most significant person arrives. Significant people can never be late, since "on time" is when they get there. One just had to wait until that central person arrived. What was required was watching and waiting in patience, not wondering what was causing the delay.[1] The death of Paul without the emergence of theocracy in Israel continued the period of watching and waiting in patience.

Thus the second generation, emerging after the significant social change of Paul's death and the need to further wait for the kingdom, found itself in tension with the new situation. The parent generation would accuse it of departing from old ways with its impatience and new customs relative to family relations and previously unheard-of theological articulations. And as might be expected, local Israelite populations among which the second generation now found itself accused it of not being Israelite enough, even by Paul's standards. The second generation was an in-between generation relative to the stable third generation. Predictably, the second generation either did not care to remember many dimensions of first-generation experience so well directed by Paul and Timothy or even wished to ignore many aspects of those experiences that their elders considered so focal.

A major ploy used by some second-generation leaders to deal with the new situation was to write new letters from Paul,

Silvanus, and Timothy to fit with their situation. This ploy could only work, of course, among Jesus-group members who once actually received letters from Paul, Silvanus, and Timothy. And given the relaxed speed of face-to-face communication over land or sea at the time, such forged letters in the name of Paul and Timothy still had plausibility. Naturally this transition generation did not really bother to remember what Paul and his aides said and did, but rather proceeded to contextualize or actualize or indigenize what it had received.

The second letter to the Thessalonians opens with the following superscription:

> Paul, Silvanus, and Timothy, To the church of the Thessalonians in God our Father and the Lord Jesus Christ: (2 Thess 1:1)

This superscription is identical to that found in the first letter to the Thessalonians. It is ascribed to the same trio who sent that letter. But 2 Thessalonians curiously tells of the existence of forgeries of Pauline letters: "either by spirit or by word or by letter purporting to be from us." The main message in those forgeries is "to the effect that the day of the Lord has come" (2 Thess 2:2). The overemphatic signed conclusion (2 Thess 3:17) is further indication that the document belongs to a generation after Paul.

The distinctive feature of this letter is the detailed teaching about the Day of the Lord and its antecedents (2 Thess 2:1-12). The "Day of the Lord" is a high-context reference to God's establishment of the new Israelite theocracy. The details concerning what would precede the Day of the Lord are an expanded and rewritten version of the advice presented by Paul, Silvanus, and Timothy in their original letter to the Thessalonians (1 Thess 5) to fit the new, second-generation situation—a form of what today is called "contextualization." The word "contextualization" derives from modern Bible translators and their task of cross-cultural communication. Here, with reference to writings from the second Pauline generation, contextualization might be described as a meaningful and appropriate cross-temporal transmission of some first-generation idea that is faithful to its original intent and sensitive to the social context of a subsequent generation. The senders of 2 Thessalonians believed that what they wrote is what Paul, Silvanus, and Timothy would have written to the second generation in its later temporal context. The senders of the letter sought to refute the idea, attributed by some to Paul and his change-agent team, that the Day of the Lord had already come. Some Jesus-group members had given up their work, a further indication of their belief (2 Thess 3:6-13). The recipients of this letter are urged to split off from those who hold otherwise (2 Thess 3:14-15). The result would be a factional power structure composed of two or more competing leadership groups in the community, one still in the Pauline tradition and the other with the newly contextualized perspective.

This second-generation experience is further indication witnessed throughout the first generations of Jesus-group development that no innovation occurs without strings attached. Here we find that one group has reinterpreted Paul's gospel of God. It has modified the gospel proclamation by dismissing the idea of Jesus' actual return from the sky. And it has reconfigured and reshaped the innovation into a mixture of ideas of immediate relevance (the kingdom is already here) and acceptable newness (give up work and wait). The senders of 2 Thessalonians find this highly flexible and adaptive interpretation to be a deviant expression of Paul's gospel. On the other hand, such deviant reinterpretation underscores the degree to which the gospel of God found success among the Thessalonians. Their acceptance of that innovation seems to have conditioned that Jesus group to accept eventual innovations, in this case the innovations decried by the senders of this letter.

In sum, the second letter to the Thessalonians has the shape of a Pauline team letter, presumably in the mold of the letter of Paul, Silvanus, and Timothy to the Thessalonians. But the voice in the letter is that of someone else, addressing second Pauline-generation problems. This second-generation letter, along with the third-generation letters to be considered in the next chapter, raises the question of forgeries in antiquity. The problem that the word "forgery" raises for modern Bible readers is the meaning attached to the word today. Nowadays forgery invariably denotes or connotes deception.

About Forgery in the Hellenistic Period

The Hellenistic Period marked a flowering of what we today would call forgeries.[2] Relative to written documents, a forgery is any piece of writing that, according to the intention of its producer(s), purports to be something other than what it really is. Hiatt observes that this description points to two key elements of the forgery: the effacement of the document's real identity and the intention of the forger to deceive.[3] The period that preceded the Hellenistic period in the Middle East is called the Persian Period.

Perhaps the most significant forgery in Western history dating to the close of the Persian Period and the beginning of the Hellenistic Period is Israel's Torah. This five-volume collection of books (Pentateuch) was ascribed to a mythical Moses and describes a fictional group of people best described as "Israel-in-the-Bible." The purpose of this set of books was to provide the diverse immigrants whom Persia settled in Yahud (Judea) with a group identity based on ancestor stories as well as to shape these immigrants into a client people for whom the image of God supported Persian imperial goals. With these recently composed writings, the Persians and their client leaders in Yahud intended to secure the loyalty of the recently arrived immigrants and their descendants through ancestor stories in which their loyalty to God/emperor demanded that they be set above and apart from the native populations.

Nowadays people for whom the Torah is sacred scripture from the ancient prophet Moses identify with the beliefs expressed in the project of the late Persian and early Hellenistic forgers and their forgery. Such modern believers would not consider the books of Moses to be a deception. "Deception" seems a rather strong term. Instead, writings considered significant or sacred forgeries are generally called "pseudepigrapha," from the Greek words *pseudēs*, meaning "lying," "false," "untrue," and *epigraphē*, meaning "superscription" or "title." A pseudepigraph is a term for a book or writing bearing a false title or ascribed to a writer other than the genuine one. For non-fundamentalists, the books of Moses in the Bible are pseudepigrapha.

It is important to recall that the categories for assessing writings as either fact or fiction are nineteenth-century categories. They followed upon the post-Enlightenment scholarly consensus that history should be about "what really happened."[4] However, such was not the shared worldview in the Hellenistic Period. In that period the evaluation of a document was not so much whether it was written by the person whose name it bore as whether the document had validity. Validation was a question of whether the document in question was duly authorized. Authorization, in turn, meant formal approval of the document, with some formal warrant or sanction. An authorized document had the social effect of commanding consent. That meant that the validity of a document derived from some agency that could authorize the document, so that it was considered worthy of consent. When it came to documents such as the Torah, the authorizing agency might be the Persian appointed high priest or court prophet. For Jesus-group writings such as the Pauline letters, the authorizing agency would be the Jesus group that agreed with the letters and kept them as special or normative in some way.

The ancient writings that modern scholars consider forgeries or falsely ascribed writings would have been quite acceptable to ancients if they were authorized, hence authoritative. For example, consider the status of the Latin translation of the Bible by Saint Jerome, called the Vulgate. Regardless of translation errors in Jerome's version, Pope Pius XII affirmed the Council of Trent's declaration that the Vulgate version is authoritative, hence authentic, although new and better versions may be made (see *Divino Afflante Spiritu*, par. 21-22).

The proper question here is whether the Jesus group and its leadership believed that the documents in question covered the problems raised by those Jesus groups in the second and third Pauline-generations. People at this stage of Jesus-group development would never preserve Pauline letters out of mere antiquarian interest. If they preserved them, that meant that the documents had authority to deal with relevant problems of the group. They were authorized, then authentic. (The word "authentic" at this time did not mean "genuine." That is later usage.)

Hiatt, who has done extensive work on medieval forgeries, makes three valuable points concerning forgeries that are just as applicable to the ancient forgeries that belong to the Pauline tradition.

A Means to Validity

First, forgeries assume the stable identity of genuine documents as a counterpoint to the unstable identity of forgeries. A forged second letter to the Thessalonians has to be pretty much just like the original first letter to the Thessalonians. One can only judge whether a document is forged if genuine documents with significantly distinctive characteristics exist. When it comes to Pauline letters, for example, they follow the stereotypical pattern of Hellenistic letters. Furthermore, letters in antiquity were normally written to assist the memory of the person who delivered them in the name of the senders. Interestingly, in the first century the phrase "in the name of" meant "taking the place of the person of," because the word "name" was the equivalent of our word "person" (for example, Acts 1:15 actually says "one hundred and twenty names," meaning one hundred and twenty persons).

Letters were actually an alternative form of face-to-face, interpersonal communication. Reciting (or reading) a letter aloud to a group was as much a form of interpersonal communication as was the gossip that invariably followed it (or preceded it, in the case of 1 Corinthians). The same was true of Paul's original proclamation of the gospel of God. By using these face-to-face, interpersonal channels of communication, the main effect sought by the change agents and their coworkers was for the recipients of the communication to adopt the change and translate the change into action. Think of the rumors that would emerge in a group experiencing the proclamation of the forthcoming arrival of the kingdom of God.[5] As the second letter to the Thessalonians indicates, some believed that "the Day of the Lord arrived." We find a similar outcome of rumor development in the Corinthian community that led to the belief that "there is no resurrection of the dead" (1 Cor 15:12), even in face of the Pauline proclamation of God's having raised Jesus from the dead as God will raise those who believe this gospel.

To get back to the face-to-face, interpersonal communication that letters were, recall the procedure involved in delivering a letter. The one delivering the letter would recite its contents to the recipients. The written form of the letter was to remind the person delivering it about what to say. Thus the highly stereotypical qualities of even genuine letters and their mode of delivery frequently rendered their origins and writers far from secure.

The Hellenistic problem with documents, then, is not one of deception, fictionality, or false identity, as these are features of many documents, genuine and forged, but rather one of authorization. The issue at stake for early Jesus-group members confronted with a possible forgery was not one of absolutes; the task was not (as it is for us) to determine the inherent truth or falsity of a document, but rather to determine its degree of validity. To use a modern example, when dealing with models of some dimension of chemistry, physics, or social life, the question is not whether the model is true or false. As abstract representations of some complex interaction, models are about approximations. There are no true or false models. (True and/or false are properties of statements or sentences). Rather, the question is whether the model is valid, and validation here consists in judging whether the model covers all the instances that it is intended to explain.

The same is true of ancient evaluations of forgeries. They were neither true nor false, but either valid or invalid. Validity in assessing ancient documents derived from authorization. And it is important to emphasize that a document could on occasion validate itself through the power—the credibility and acceptability—of its discourse or narrative. For example, Muslims are certain that the Qur'an is God's direct word because of the beauty of its language (called *ijaz*). Such beauty surpasses human ability. The text is therefore self-validating.[6] There is nothing of such beauty in any Old or New Testament writing. The validation of these writings must derive from elsewhere.

A Means to Textualization

The second point to make about the usual definition of forgery is that it leaves out the forgery's audience. If a defining feature of the forgery is the malicious intention of the forger, the will of the forger to deceive, then the expectations and response of the audience or receivers of the forged document are equally important. One must take into account the degree of collusion that may exist between producer and reader. As Hiatt has duly noted, often the purpose of forgeries was

> not to deceive a hostile or unsuspecting audience, but to document an already accepted state of affairs, to explain a set of circumstances, to add substance to myth, or to express in the form of official written record narratives that existed in unofficial or semi-official sources. At times such activities did involve an element of deception, but often the role of the forgery was to satisfy the need or desire for a text of age and authority—a text that could be accepted without dispute. This was not, simply, a case of "mundus vult decipi, ergo decipiatur" [people wish to be deceived, so let them be deceived]. The world did not want to be deceived; it wanted to be textualised.[7]

This feature is especially apparent for nascent Yahud and its sacred writing (Torah) during the early Hellenistic Period. Some dimensions of it likewise hold for letters of the second and third Pauline generations.

The features that would allay any dispute about the validity of 2 Thessalonians, Colossians, Ephesians, and the Pastorals (1–2 Timothy, Titus) would be: (1) the letters were said to be sent by and directed to very well-known communities and personages, well known within Pauline Jesus groups, and (2) the sender or senders were presumed to be alive by the forgers at the time of writing. Then in the communities that accepted these letters, (3) they had to sound like Paul, Timothy, or other Pauline change agents sounded to them. These letters presumably "textualized," with the approval of Paul (or his team), the behaviors in vogue in those groups. While we might think the second point (the senders were alive) might be readily verified, such would not have been the situation in antiquity, given the geographical restrictions on easy information retrieval.

A Means to Analysis

The third point Hiatt makes is that the "producer" of the forgery is usually an anonymous figure, a corporate sender (as was the case with most of Paul's letters, genuine or not). The identity of the forger is frequently absent of necessity from the analysis of documents forged. The advantage of anonymity, the absence of any ready access to the identity or intentions of those who produced forged texts, requires that we focus attention on the texts themselves. They have to be read as discourses or narratives that circulated within a community that valued written documents, documents that can be validated or rejected by community members, and hence that indicate the kinds of texts valued or required by the community. While these points are quite on target for the letters of the second and third Pauline generations, the same held true for those anonymous documents known as the Gospels of Matthew, Mark, Luke and John, anonymous writers all.

These reflections on forgery should be coupled with several observations of a social historical sort. First of all, ascribing anonymous documents to Paul, Silvanus, and Timothy or to Paul and Timothy or to Paul alone certifies the content of the message and gives it weight and a personal seal, so to say. The careers and reputations of the persons named as writers are linked with the earliest phase of Jesus-group development among Israelites in non-Israelite cities. Their change-agent activity in the northeastern region of the Mediterranean and their concern for the fictive-kin Jesus groups in Asia Minor, Macedonia, and Achaia illustrates God's abiding interest in and concern for all Israel, even those far from Jerusalem. The roots of the activity and of the letters of the Pauline team in the greater house of Israel of the first-century Mediterranean Diaspora explain the rich diversity of the traditions, Judean and Greek, that developed in these groups.

Of course, Paul was the chief and central figure of the change-agent team indelibly associated with these letters. Yet even the anonymous Luke, the first biographer of Paul, would have us dismiss the "big man" view of history, according to which single (male!) individuals affected the course of events. This view, again a figment of the nineteenth-century imagination, simply belies the presence of collaborators such as Timothy, Silvanus, and Sosthenes, to name only the co-senders of the Pauline letters. In any event, in a collectivistic world, if Paul had impact on Israelites living in predominantly non-Israelite regions, and in this way spread the gospel of the God of Israel throughout the northeastern Mediterranean, such an outcome had to be the result of a working group. For it could only have been persuasive and powerful groups leading collective movements that altered this phase of the course of Israel's history.

We might mention again the common misapprehension according to which people call Paul the second founder of Christianity, with Jesus obviously the founder. Yet as far as the New Testament documents are concerned, both Jesus and Paul insist that they responded to the command of the God of Israel. The

God of Israel, according to their witness, is the founder of what would become "Christianity." As the Jesus movement advanced beyond Palestine, it grew in strength through the formation of teams of change agents and innovator/first adopter support groups that entailed the assimilation of households and the establishment of social networks. The same was true of other Jesus-group change agents such as Barnabas and Mark, Aquila and Prisca, and Apollo and Peter. They all had their groups of associates, coworkers, aides, and supporters.

While Jesus was remembered as a prophet and a holy man, like John the Baptist, who proclaimed the forthcoming kingdom of heaven, a new Israelite theocracy, and while this feature was crucial to early Jesus-group formation, yet it was not Jesus' main claim to remembrance. That feature was the witnessed fact that the God of Israel raised Jesus from the dead, thus validating his proclamation of theocracy to Israel. This remembrance was duly shared by Paul and his associates, a God-appointed change-agent team commissioned to proclaim the gospel of the God of Israel to Israelites resident in non-Israelite majority cities. Like God's first-ranked change agent to Israel and as proper collectivistic person, Jesus too recruited a change-agent team to assist him in his God-commissioned task. And so did Paul, as his collaborative letters indicate.

Among Paul's coworkers, Timothy stands out. The fact that there are two letters to Timothy that emerged in the third Pauline generation (to be considered in the next chapter) indicates the prestige level that Timothy and his memory enjoyed in those generations following his activity. The information they offer about his family and his youth are typical of third generations' remembering of a central ancestor in faith. Whether the data are true or not is beside the point for those who commemorate his activity. They simply are valid and worthy of textualization.

CHAPTER 7

Final Traditions about Timothy
in the New Testament

In this final chapter we will consider the third generation-Pauline letter ascribed to Paul and Timothy as co-senders as well as Paul's letters to Timothy. Of course, these letters are pseudepigrapha or forgeries, as explained in the previous chapter (see pp. 114ff.). What they present are textualized versions of the traditions of the Pauline Jesus groups. They share the memories of their ancestors in faith that these group members cherished as well as contextualized versions of the Pauline teaching.

The third-generation letter to the Jesus group at Colossae, ascribed to Paul and Timothy, has the following superscription:

> Paul, an apostle of Christ Jesus by the will of God, and Timothy our brother. (Col 1:1)

This superscription is identical with that in 2 Cor 1:1. The letter to the Colossians states that the Jesus group in the Hellenistic city of Colossae was founded by a person named Epaphras (Col 1:7), obviously another Jesus-group change agent. Paul and Timothy here call Epaphras "our beloved fellow slave" (RSV:

"servant"). This description would have the recipients of this letter at Colossae believe that Paul and Timothy write in support of Epaphras's change-agent activity in order to support the Colossians in their innovation decision and to dissuade any discontinuance. The main discordant point casting doubt on the authenticity of the letter is that in the genuine letters Paul and collaborators insist that Paul does not bother with "work already done in another's field" (2 Cor 10:16), nor did he build on another man's foundation (Rom 15:20). If Paul and Timothy did not found the Jesus group at Colossae, why a letter in their name?

Obviously, the forgers wished to have the authority of Paul and Timothy, the great change agents among Israelites living among non-Israelites, to influence the Jesus group to whom the letter is directed. We learn in the letter that group members have been besieged by proponents of a Judean ideology that would have the Colossians take up the Torah practices presented to Moses after the incident of the golden calf: kosher foods, Torah calendar and feasts, with sabbath observances, fasting, and the worship of angels (Col 2:16-18). The sender describes these proponents as purveyors of "philosophy and empty deceit, according to human tradition, according to the elemental spirits of the universe, and not according to Christ" (Col 2:8). While Paul and Timothy may have faced such Judean opposition, the sender's way of dealing with it is quite different from Paul's, for example in the letter to the Galatians.

Furthermore, in the letter of Paul and Sosthenes to the Corinthians, the entire Jesus group itself is designated as the body of Christ: "Now you are the body of Christ and individually members of it" (1 Cor 12:27). In this letter Jesus is "the head of the body" (Col 1:18; 2:19), a rather different image in which Jesus members form the torso of Christ. Moreover, the description of Jesus as head of all heads in whom "the whole fullness of deity dwells bodily" (Col 2:10-11) is an indication of a new contextualization.

Furthermore, Paul's phrase in Gal 3:27-29, with which he concludes his argument about Christ Jesus as Abraham's offspring, heir of God's promise, thanks to faith in God without works of the law, is likewise recontextualized. The traditional baptism ideology sees all who have been baptized into Christ as having undergone a transformative event, a social putting on of Christ. In Col 3:11 the outcome is Christ becoming all in all, not the Galatians' emphasis of Jesus-group members having become one in Christ. Yet the point in Colossians is that Israelite Jesus-group members of whatever social category, whether Judean or Hellenist, whether circumcised or uncircumcised, whether barbarian or Scythian (really another barbarian group), whether slave or free, have Christ all in all. The literary parallelism in this presentation is a bit botched, further departing from Pauline usage.

Finally, the letter to the Colossians offers a rather lengthy exhortation concerning the proper attitudes and behavior required of group members within their family circles. Biblical scholars have often called these "household codes" (Col 3:22–4:1; and later in Eph 6:5-9; *Epistle of Barnabas* 19.7; *Didache* 4.10-11). These codes describe Jesus-group members who are heads of households as really subordinates of another Lord, while household slaves must behave as moral agents. The values laid out in the codes are the well-known Greco-Roman household themes of justice, accountability, and piety made known in elite circles through ancient handbooks on agriculture.[1]

Furthermore, in this letter Paul is described as still in prison and would have the Colossians see to having this letter read in Laodicea and Hierapolis (Col 4:10-16), making it a sort of circular letter. Perhaps because of this letter from Paul and Timothy, with Paul imprisoned with a certain Aristarchus (Col 4:10), the anonymous writer of the tract called the letter to the Hebrews believes that Timothy was in prison too. That tract concludes with "You should understand that our brother Timothy has been released, with whom I shall see you if he comes soon" (Heb 13:23). There really is no clue to who the "I" might be, and the document does not have the form of a letter, although later tradition makes of Hebrews a "letter of the apostle Paul."

On the other hand, the treatise entitled "To the Hebrews" does share an interest so well articulated in Colossians, specifically in the great hymn of Col 1:15-23 on the present role of the resurrected Jesus. There is a similar interest expressed in Eph 1:20-23. These all sound like third Pauline-generation Jesus-groups writings, sharing the overwhelming concern of this generation: What is the exalted Jesus doing now as we await the establishment of a theocracy in Israel? Colossians and Ephesians describe Jesus as exalted Lord; Hebrews describes him as Israel's true High Priest in the sky. While the general Pauline tradition of the theme of the forthcoming Israelite kingdom of God endures right on to the third Pauline generation, that theme is more of a whisper now than the centerpiece of the gospel of God that it was for Paul, Timothy, and their generation.

The second letter to the Thessalonians and the letter to the Colossians underscore the significance and authority of Paul and Timothy among members of later Pauline generations. The concerns of these generations have shifted, and the innovation proclaimed by Paul and Timothy has been reinterpreted and recontextualized.

Paul to Timothy

The letters labeled the first and second letters to Timothy present a picture of Timothy as a type of the ideal Jesus-group leader. Scholars using historical and philological methods all date these documents (along with the letter to Titus) to a period toward the turn of the first century.[2] From another point of view, we can date them to the third Pauline generation, for given the interests expressed in these letters about the life of Paul and the person of Timothy, along with data about their lives, we can situate them as belonging to the third post-Pauline generation using the principle of third-generation interest (see chap. 2, pp. 23ff.).

We know from the Pauline letters that Timothy accompanied Paul and collaborated with him as a change-agent aide from the time of Paul's first reported incursion into Thessalonika to the time he wrote the recommendation appended to the letter to the Romans. The writer of Acts names Timothy among those who were with Paul before he left on his final trip to Jerusalem (Acts 20:4). This means that Timothy was Paul's coworker for a whole generation of adult activity. In other words, if Timothy were alive at the time these third generation-Pauline letters to Timothy were written, he would not be a young man at all. Yet these letters address him as a rather young person with very little field experience, so to say. This would be the wrong Timothy, an anachronistic Timothy. This feature would have scholars situate these letters, often called the Pastoral Letters (see below), among inauthentic letters of Paul.

In sum, as already noted, the letters to Timothy and Titus are forgeries. Their main use for a life of Timothy is the fact that they present remembrances of Timothy largely based on recollections of the sort of person Timothy must have been and therefore was. This is what such well-accepted forgeries do, as noted in the previous chapter.

Timothy-Titus as Letters from a Third Generation-Pauline Jesus Group in Ephesus

We have already seen that Paul, like other Jesus-group change agents and Jesus himself, worked in groups or teams with the assistance of collaborators. This feature typical of collectivist cultures is well documented from the authentic Pauline letters. It is also highly likely on the basis of cross-cultural study of the communication of innovation. Change agents have coworkers usually chosen from among innovators and first adopters. In the process of spreading an innovation, the experiences, thoughts, visions, and actions of one person become socially relevant and effective only when they are shared by a group or groups of sympathizers. Of the change-agent coworkers noted in the authentic Pauline letters, Timothy and Titus stand out both because of their attested activities during Paul's career and because they have been singled out in traditions about Paul by having third Pauline-generation letters addressed to them.

The letters to Timothy and Titus are called "pastoral" letters, or the Pastorals. The word "pastoral" comes from Latin, where it means of or pertaining to a shepherd. The Mediterranean shepherds' role was used as an analogy for the role of Jesus-group managers. They are often called "leaders," but in fact they are like managers, since in the patriarchal culture of the ancient Mediterranean, they did not have the power of legal family heads or patriarchs. Rather their role was like that of a maternal uncle, the mother's brother in patriarchal systems, who was attached to her children because they were attached to her.

The distinction between relatives on the father's side and the mother's side was and is very significant in patriarchal societies, with special names for each status (for example: the mother's brother in medieval English was *Em*, in German *Oheim*, in Polish *wuja*, in ancient Latin *avunculus*, and in Greek *mētrōs*; the father's brother in the "powerline" was called *Uncle* in English, *Onkel* in German, *stryj* in Polish, *patruus* in Latin, and *patrōs* in Greek). The mother's brother had no rights or entitlements relative to his sister's family.

The same was true of the central persons in the fictive kinship Jesus groups at the time of Timothy, called "supervisors" (Greek: *episkopoi*, often translated as "bishop"). They really had no rights or entitlements over group members, since membership was not required or forced by any institutional statute or law. Hence success in their way of managing Jesus groups depended solely in interpersonal competence. For people might join a Jesus group or leave it without fear of legal sanctions.

This whole situation would change with the advent of political Christianity, called Christendom, with Emperor Constantine and his successors. With the advent of Christendom, bishops took on political authority, and deviation from the group, called "heresy," became a political crime, with sanctions from the "state." This is an important feature to keep in mind when discussing ancient Jesus-group organization, since the patriarchal features many people find in those organizations actually derive from the post-Constantine church.

The fact that Timothy and Titus have such letters addressed to them attests to the prestige of their memory. This was something third Pauline-generation forgers could count on when they chose them as ideal "supervisors." For Timothy, these letters are localized at Ephesus and surrounding region (1 Tim 1:3; 2 Tim 1:18; 4:12), while for Titus, the locale mentioned is Crete (Titus 1:5; see Acts 27). While that other third Pauline-generation document, the Acts of the Apostles, does not mention Titus at all, it does single out Ephesus by noting that Paul's final speech was addressed to the Ephesian Jesus-group elders (the speech was delivered at Miletus, the last of Paul's stopovers before he undertook a final trip to Jerusalem). In effect, the story of Paul's change-agent travels ends with Ephesian Jesus-group members, Acts 20:21-35.

As might be expected, these third Pauline-generation documents provide information about Paul and Timothy about which the second Pauline generation was not concerned. First of all, we are briefly told how and why Paul became a change agent of the innovation of God's gospel (1 Tim 1:12–2:8). The rest of the letter sets out Paul's instructions for Timothy, who was to remain at Ephesus (1 Tim 1:3), effectively marking the close of his career as change-agent coworker. Instead, he is to act as a local supervisor. The Paul of this letter indicates that Timothy is "my child" and destined for this present task by "prophecies made earlier about you" (1 Tim 1:18).

There is even more about Paul and his travels and motivations in the second letter (2 Tim 3:10–4:18). And as might be expected in a narrative about significant persons, later traditions tend to provide names to persons who were earlier anonymous. Thus we learn about the names of Timothy's mother (Eunice) and grandmother (Lois) in 2 Tim 1:5, from whom he presumably learned Israel's sacred writings so well from childhood (2 Tim 3:15). The women both have Hellenistic names, even though Luke claims that Eunice was a Judean (Acts 16:1).

Both letters offer specific and general information concerning the Ephesian Jesus groups of the third Pauline generation. Specifically, individuals are named as inimical to the group: Hymenaeus and Alexander (1 Tim 2:20), who are accused of rejecting Jesus-group consensus; and again Hymenaeus and Philetus (2 Tim 2:17), who claimed that the resurrection had already taken place; Alexander (2 Tim 4:14), who strongly opposed Paul's message; Phygelus and Hermogenes (2 Tim 1:15), who discontinued the innovation they once adopted. The close of 2 Timothy (4:9-21) lists a whole set of persons, some known from the authentic Pauline letters, others not. This proliferation of personal names both indicates third-generation concerns and serves the needs of this third generation Pauline-Jesus group.

The general information in these letters deals with Jesus-group beliefs and behaviors. Among beliefs we might note the reworking of Israel's profession of faith: "There is one God, there is one mediator between God and men, the man Christ Jesus, who gave himself as a ransom for all" (1 Tim 2:5-6, which parallels the Shema of Deut 6:4: "Hear, O Israel, the Lord our God, the Lord is one"). Then there is the hymn about Jesus Christ: "He was manifested in the flesh, vindicated in the Spirit, seen by angels, preached among the nations, believed on in the world, taken up in glory" (1 Tim 3:16).

About behaviors, the letters are notable for advice on married women (1 Tim 2:8-15) and widows (1 Tim 5:9-16) and other social categories, and especially for a description of qualities that befit a Jesus-group supervisor or bishop (1 Tim 3:1-7), a description that is very close to the description of qualities desirable in a Roman general (from Onosander, *De imperatoris officio*[3]). And both letters urge against deception by false teachers (1 Tim 6:3-10; 2 Tim 3:1-9).

The letters to Timothy honor him by having these letters addressed to him and thereby assure him a significant place in the traditions shared by Pauline Jesus groups. For modern scholars, these letters are of far more value for an understanding of what was going on in the third Pauline-generation Jesus groups at Ephesus and surrounding region. The letters more than amply prove that innovations, even those proclaimed by Paul and his team, will be reinterpreted and contextualized by later adapters, even those in the Pauline tradition from birth. They also demonstrate that a change agent's task will always end with a termination of the relationship by having some local person take over. For these Jesus groups, it was the local or sedentary supervisor (or bishop), the traveling change agent's successor.

CONCLUSION

This summary study of the life of Timothy has been based largely on what is known of first-century Mediterranean persons in general and on the information from New Testament documents. Timothy was a collaborator of Paul and a cowriter of several Pauline letters. He was a collectivistic person, devoted to the Jesus-groups that he helped found and support by his presence and direction. As a collaborator of Paul and the Pauline team, he was a second-generation Jesus-group member, a "Greek," or a civilized and educated person at home in the Israelite communities of non-Israelite majority cities in the northeastern Mediterranean. His task was to proclaim Paul's gospel of God: that the God of Israel raised Jesus of Nazareth from the dead, indicating that this Jesus was Lord and Israel's Messiah, with a view to a forthcoming Israelite theocracy in Jerusalem. His gospel of the God of Israel, like Paul's, was for Israelites resident in non-Israelite majority cities.

Timothy followed his change-agent career in its various tasks, much as Paul did. Aside from developing a need for change among Israelites by proclaiming the gospel of God with Paul and Silvanus, Timothy was crucial in maintaining an information-exchange relationship with Pauline Jesus groups. He diagnosed problems, created intent to change and to translate this intent into action, and worked to stabilize and prevent discontinuance.

Timothy was significant enough to be highlighted in second and third Pauline-generation Jesus groups in a number of forgeries. The canonical letters to Timothy hallowed his presence at Ephesus by remembering him as local supervisor (bishop). And it was as bishop of Ephesus that Timothy has been commemorated in subsequent Christian tradition.[1] In sum, if Paul was a significant presence in the story of second-generation Jesus groups, Timothy surely was important enough to merit great attention as well.

NOTES

Note to Introduction (pages ix–xvi)

1. It is very useful to use an appropriate map when considering the travels of Paul, Timothy, and others. If you find a historically accurate map, you will notice that there is no region called "Greece" in the first century. For example, see *Barrington Atlas of the Greek and Roman World*, edited by Richard J. A. Talbert, in collaboration with Roger S. Bagnall, et al.; and map editors Mary E. Downs, M. Joann McDaniel; cartographic managers, Janet E. Kelly, Jeannine M. Schonta, David F. Stong (Princeton, NJ: Princeton Univ. Press, 2000).

Notes to Chapter 1 (pages 1–20)

1. Clifford Geertz, "'From the Native's Point of View': On the Nature of Anthropological Understanding," in Keith H. Basso and Henry A. Selby, eds., *Meaning and Anthropology*, 221–37 (Albuquerque: University of New Mexico Press, 1976).

2. Harry C. Triandis, "Cross-Cultural Studies in Individualism and Collectivism," in R. A. Diensbier and J. J. Berman, eds., *Nebraska Symposium on Motivation 1989*, 41–133 (Lincoln: University of Nebraska Press, 1990).

3. Geert H. Hofstede, *Culture's Consequences: International Differences in Work-Related Values*, Cross-Cultural Research and Methodology Series 5 (Beverly Hills, CA, et alibi: Sage Publications, 1984); Geert H. Hofstede, *Culture's Consequences: Comparing Values, Behaviors, Institutions, and Organizations Across Nations*, 2nd ed. (Thousand Oaks, CA: Sage, 2001).

4. Arthur M. Kleinman, "Concepts and a Model for the Comparison of Medical Systems," in Cariline Currer and Meg Stacey, eds., *Concepts of Health, Illness and Disease: A Comparative Perspective*, 29–47 (New York: Berg,

1986); John J. Pilch, "Altered States of Consciousness in the Synoptics," in Wolfgang Stegemann, Bruce J. Malina, and Gerd Theissen, eds., *The Social Setting of Jesus and The Gospels*, 103–15 (Minneapolis: Fortress Press, 2002).

5. See Bruce J. Malina, "Dealing with Biblical (Mediterranean) Characters: A Guide for U.S. Consumers," *Biblical Theology Bulletin* 19 (1989): 127–14; Bruce J. Malina, "Is There a Circum-Mediterranean Person: Looking for Stereotypes," *Biblical Theology Bulletin* 22 (1992): 66–87.

6. Edward T. Hall, *Beyond Culture* (Garden City, NY: Doubleday and Company, 1976); Edward T. Hall, *The Dance of Life: The Other Dimensions of Time* (Garden City, NY: Doubleday and Company, 1983).

7. According to a 2002 poll by the Barna organization, more than 70 percent of Americans believe that they have no need for any other information to understand the Bible apart from their own reading of the English translation. George Barna, *The State of the Church, 2002* (Ventura, CA: Issachar Resources, 2002).

8. Triandis, "Cross-Cultural Studies in Individualism and Collectivism," 77–78.

9. William G. Sumner, *Folkways: a Study of the Sociological Importance of Usages, Manners, Customs, Mores, and Morals* (Boston: Ginn, 1906).

10. Triandis, "Cross-Cultural Studies in Individualism and Collectivism."

11. In the contemporary world, societies based on collectivistic cultures have low rates of homicide, suicide, crime, juvenile delinquency, divorce, child abuse, wife beating, and drug and alcohol abuse and are characterized by good mental health. On the other hand, such societies are also characterized by dissatisfaction with the excessive demands of family life, by low gross national product per capita, and by the poor functioning of the overall society in the political realm. Thus there is a trade-off between quality of private and public life, which are kept quite separate. And we might expect something of the sort in ancient collectivistic societies, such as those in which Timothy and his fellows lived.

12. Harry C. Triandis, *Individualism and Collectivism*, New Directions in Social Psychology (San Francisco: Westview, 1995).

13. See Richard L. Rohrbaugh, "Ethnocentrism and the Historical Questions about Jesus," in Wolfgang Stegemann, Bruce J. Malina, and Gerd Theissen, eds., *The Social Setting of Jesus and the Gospels*, 27–44 (Minneapolis: Fortress Press, 2002).

Notes to Chapter 2 (pages 21–47)

1. See Hayden White, *Metahistory: The Historical Imagination in Nineteenth Century Europe* (Baltimore: Johns Hopkins University Press, 1973); for Paul

and Timothy, see Wilhelm Michaelis, *Die Gefangenschaft des Paulus in Ephesus und das Itinerar des Timotheus. Untersuchungen zur Chronologie des Paulus und der Paulusbriefe*, Neutestamentliche Forschungen 3 (Gütersloh: Bertelsmann, 1925); Robert Jewett, *A Chronology of Paul's Life* (Philadelphia: Fortress Press, 1979); Gregory Tatum, *New Chapters in the Life of Paul: The Relative Chronology of His Career*, Catholic Biblical Quarterly Monographs 41 (Washington: Catholic Biblical Association, 2006).

2. Marcus L. Hansen, *The Problem of the Third Generation Immigrant*, Augustana Historical Society Publications 8 (Rock Island, IL: Augustana Historical Society, 1938).

3. Will Herberg, *Protestant-Catholic-Jew: An Essay in American Religious Sociology* (Garden City, NY: Doubleday, 1955).

4. Eusebius, *Historia Ecclesiastica*, H.E.III.39, cited from Philip Schaff and Henry Wace, eds., *A Select Library of Nicene and Post-Nicene Fathers of the Christian Church*, 2nd series, vol. 1 (Grand Rapids, MI: W. B. Eerdmans, 1952), 170–71.

5. Bruce J. Malina and Richard L. Rohrbaugh, *Social Science Commentary on the Synoptic Gospels*, 2nd ed. (Minneapolis: Fortress Press, 2003), 409–12.

6. See Bruce J. Malina and John J. Pilch, *Social Science Commentary on the Letters of Paul* (Minneapolis: Fortress Press, 2006), 1–25.

7. On shift from temple to household, see John H. Elliott, "Temple versus Household in Luke-Acts: A Contrast in Social Institutions," in Jerome H. Neyrey, ed., *The Social World of Luke-Acts: Models for Interpretation* (Peabody, MA: Hendrickson, 1991), 211–40.

8. Bruce J. Malina, "Christ and Time: Swiss or Mediterranean," *Catholic Biblical Quarterly* 51 (1989): 1–31. Reprinted in Bruce J. Malina, *The Social World of Jesus and the Gospels* (New York/London: Routledge, 1996), 179–214.

9. Hansen, *The Problem of the Third Generation Immigrant*, 10.

10. About the visionaries in Acts, see John J. Pilch, *Visions and Healings in the Acts of the Apostles: How the Early Believers Experienced God* (Collegeville, MN: Liturgical Press, 2004). Eucharistic Prayer I of the Roman Mass alludes to such experiences; see Giles Quispel, "The *Asclepius*: From the Hermetic Lodge in Alexandria to the Greek Eucharist and the Roman Mass," in Roelof van den Broek and Wouter J. Hanegraaff, eds., *Gnosis and Hermeticism from Antiquity to Modern Times* (Albany: SUNY Press, 1998), 69–78.

11. See David E. Aune, *Revelation*, Word Commentary 1 (Dallas: Word Books, 1997); Laurence H. Kant, "Jewish Inscriptions in Greek and Latin," *Aufstieg und Niedergang der römischen Welt: Geschichte und Kultur Roms im Spiegel der neueren Forschung*, II 20, 2, ed. H. Temporini and W. Haase (Berlin/New York: De Gruyter, 1987), 617–713; Edrei, Arye and Doron Mendels, "A Split Jewish Diaspora: Its Dramatic Consequences," *Journal for the Study of the Pseudepigrapha* 16.2 (2007) 91–137.

12. Hansen, *The Problem of the Third Generation Immigrant,* 10.

13. Charles H. Talbert, *Literary Patterns, Theological Themes, and the Genre of Luke-Acts,* Society of Biblical Literature 1974 (Missoula, MT: Scholars' Press, 1975).

14. See Malina, "Christ and Time."

Notes to Chapter 3 (pages 48–69)

1. John J. Pilch, *Visions and Healings in the Acts of the Apostles: How the Early Believers Experienced God* (Collegeville, MN: Liturgical Press, 2004).

2. See Bruce J. Malina and John J. Pilch, *Social Science Commentary on the Letters of Paul* (Minneapolis: Fortress Press, 2006), 1–25.

3. The models come from Everett M. Rogers with Lynne Svenning, *Modernization Among Peasants: The Impact of Communication* (New York: Holt, Rinehart and Winston, 1969); Everett M. Rogers with F. Floyd Shoemaker, *Communication of Innovations: A Cross-Cultural Approach,* 2nd ed. (New York: Free Press, 1971); Everett M. Rogers, *Diffusion of Innovations,* 4th ed. (New York: Free Press, 1995); see his bibliographies for comparative data.

4. See Richard L. Rohrbaugh, "Gossip in the New Testament," in John J. Pilch, ed., *Social Science Models for Interpeting the Bible: Essays by the Context Group in Honor of Bruce J. Malina,* Biblical Interpretation Series 53 (Leiden: Brill, 2001), 239–59.

5. See the works of Everett M. Rogers cited in note 3 above.

6. Such were envoys, for example; see Margaret M. Mitchell, "New Testament Envoys in the Context of Greco-Roman Diplomatic and Epistolary Conventions: The Example of Timothy and Titus," *Journal of Biblical Literature* 111 (1992): 641–62. Timothy and Titus were not such envoys.

7. See Henry Chadwick and G. R. Evans, eds., *Atlas of the Christian Church* (London: Macmillan, 1987).

8. See Jeremy Boissevain, *Friends of Friends: Networks, Manipulators, and Coalitions* (New York: St. Martin's Press, 1974).

9. See Bruce J. Malina, *The Social Gospel of Jesus: The Kingdom of God in Mediterranean Perspective* (Minneapolis: Fortress Press, 2001).

Notes to Chapter 4 (pages 70–94)

1. See Paul Veyne, "*Humanitas*: Romans and Non-Romans," in *The Romans,* ed. Andrea Giardina, trans. Lydia G. Cochrane (Chicago: University of

Chicago Press, 1993), 342–69; N. Petrochilos, *Roman Attitudes to the Greeks* (Athens: Kovanis, 1974); F. W. Walbank, "The Problem of Greek Nationality," in Thomas Harrison, ed., *Greeks and Barbarians* (New York: Routledge, 2002), 234–56.

2. Robert Jewett, "Tenement Churches and Communal Meals in the Early Church: The Implications of a Form Critical Analysis of 2 Thessalonians 3:10," *Biblical Research* 38 (1993): 23–42.

3. See Gustav Hermansen, *Ostia: Aspects of Roman City Life* (Edmonton: University of Alberta Press, 1982) for photos of upper-status non-elite dwellings in first-century Ostia.

4. Ramón Trevijano Etcheverría, "Los Viajes de Timoteo y la secuencia de las cartas paulinas," *Estudios Bíblicos* 57 (1999): 683–709.

5. See, for example, Margaret Mitchell, "New Testament Envoys in the Context of Greco-Roman Diplomatic and Epistolary Conventions: The Example of Timothy and Titus," *Journal of Biblical Literature* 111 (1992): 641–62.

6. See Dennis C. Duling, *The New Testament: History, Literature, and Social Context*, 4th ed. (Wadsworth: Thomson, 2003).

7. See M. Eugene Boring, Klaus Berger, and Carsten Colpe, eds., *Hellenistic Commentary to the New Testament* (Nashville: Abingdon, 1995).

8. For these studies, once again see Everett M. Rogers with Lynne Svenning, *Modernization Among Peasants: The Impact of Communication* (New York: Holt, Rinehart and Winston, 1969); Everett M. Rogers with F. Floyd Shoemaker, *Communication of Innovations: A Cross-Cultural Approach*, 2nd ed. (New York: Free Press, 1971); Everett M. Rogers, *Diffusion of Innovations*, 4th ed. (New York: Free Press, 1995); see his bibliographies for comparative data.

Notes to Chapter 5 (pages 95–109)

1. Arnaldo Momigliano, *Alien Wisdom: The Limits of Hellenization* (Cambridge: Cambridge University Press, 1975).

2. Shaye Cohen, "'Those Who Say They Are Jews and Are Not': How Do You Know a Jew in Antiquity When You See One?" in Shaye Cohen and Ernest Frerichs, eds., *Diasporas in Antiquity*, Brown Judaic Studies 288 (Atlanta: Scholars, 1993), 13.

3. N. Rubin, "Mšykt 'wrlh wtqnt hpry'h [On Drawing Down the Prepuce and Incision of the Foreskin—Peri'ah])," *Zion* (Jerusalem) 54, no. 1 (1989): 105–17.

4. See Bruce J. Malina and Jerome H. Neyrey, *Portraits of Paul: An Archaeology of Ancient Personality* (Louisville: Westminster/John Knox, 1996).

Notes to Chapter 6 (pages 101–121)

1. See Bruce J. Malina, "Christ and Time: Swiss or Mediterranean," *Catholic Biblical Quarterly* 51 (1989): 1–31. Reprinted in Bruce J. Malina, *The Social World of Jesus and the Gospels* (New York/London: Routledge, 1996), 179–214.

2. The Hellenistic Period in the eastern Mediterranean, the period when language, behavior, and outlook took on a "Greek" stamp that merited the label of civilized and well-educated, also covered what political historians call the early Roman Period. To be "Greek" meant to be civilized, not barbarian. Elite Romans claimed to be "Greek," and Greek was the cultured language of those Israelite Jesus groups that produced the New Testament narratives called "Gospels." It was also the language of Jesus groups in Rome well into the period of the establishment of Christendom. This occurred with Emperor Constantine in the early fourth century AD, when Christianity emerged as a political religion; see Paul Veyne, "*Humanitas*: Romans and Non-Romans," in *The Romans*, ed. Andrea Giardina, trans. Lydia G. Cochrane (Chicago: University of Chicago Press, 1993), 342–69.

3. Alfred Hiatt, *The Making of Medieval Forgeries: False Documents in Fifteenth-Century England* (Toronto: British Museum/University of Toronto Press, 2004).

4. See Stephen Prickett, *Origins of Narrative: The Romantic Appropriation of the Bible* (Cambridge: University Press, 1996).

5. See Richard L. Rohrbaugh, "Gossip in the New Testament," in John J. Pilch, ed., *Social Science Models for Interpeting the Bible: Essays by the Context Group in Honor of Bruce J. Malina*, Biblical Interpretation Series 53 (Leiden: Brill, 2001), 239–59.

6. See Ismail K. Poonawala, "An Ismaili Treatise on the Ijaz al-Qur'an," *Journal of the American Oriental Society* 108 (1988): 379–85.

7. Hiatt, *The Making of Medieval Forgeries*, 14.

Notes to Chapter 7 (pages 122–130)

1. See J. Albert Harrill, *Slaves in the New Testament: Literary, Social, and Moral Dimensions* (Minneapolis: Fortress Press, 2006).

2. For opposing views, see Michael Prior, *Paul the Letter Writer and the Second Letter to Timothy*, Journal for the Study of the New Testament, Supp. 23 (Sheffield: JSOT Press, 1989).

3. Cited at length by Martin Dibelius and Hans Conzelmann, *The Pastoral Epistles: A Commentary on the Pastoral Epistles*, ed. Helmut Koester, trans.

Philip Buttolph and Adela Yarbro, (Minneapolis: Fortress Press, 1972), 158–60.

Note to Conclusion (pages 131–132)

1. For a collection of early ancient documents, see Joannes Carnandet, ed., *Acta sanctorum quotquot toto orbe coluntur*, vol. 3, Jan. 24 (Paris: Victor Palme, 1863).

BIBLIOGRAPHY

Aune, David E. *Revelation*. Word Commentary. Vol. 1. Dallas: Word Books, 1997.

Beatrice, Pier Franco. "Forgery, Propaganda and Power in Christian Antiquity." *Jahrbuch für Antike und Christentum* 33 (2002): 41–51.

Boissevain, Jeremy. *Friends of Friends: Networks, Manipulators, and Coalitions*. New York: St. Martin's Press, 1974.

Chadwick, Henry, and G. R. Evans, eds. *Atlas of the Christian Church*. London: Macmillan, 1987.

Cohen, Shaye. 1993. "'Those Who Say They Are Jews and Are Not': How Do You Know a Jew in Antiquity When You See One?" In *Diasporas in Antiquity*, edited by Shaye Cohen and Ernest Frerichs, 1–46. Brown Judaic Studies 288. Atlanta: Scholars Press, 1993.

———. *The Beginnings of Jewishness: Boundaries, Varieties, Uncertainties*. Berkeley: University of California Press, 1999.

Dibelius, Martin, and Hans Conzelmann. *The Pastoral Epistles: A Commentary on the Pastoral Epistles*. Edited by Helmut Koester. Translated by Philip Buttolph and Adela Yarbro. Minneapolis: Fortress Press, 1972.

Duling, Dennis C. *The New Testament: History, Literature, and Social Context*. 4th ed. Wadsworth: Thomson, 2003.

Edrei, Arye and Doron Mendels. "A Split Jewish Diaspora: Its Dramatic Consequences." *Journal for the Study of the Pseudepigrapha* 16.2 (2007) 91–137.

Elliott, John H. "Temple versus Household in Luke-Acts: A Contrast in Social Institutions." In *The Social World of Luke-Acts: Models for Interpretation*, edited by Jerome H. Neyrey, 211–40. Peabody, MA: Hendrickson, 1991.

Geertz, Clifford. "'From the Native's Point of View': On the Nature of Anthropological Understanding." In *Meaning and Anthropology*, edited by Keith H. Basso and Henry A. Selby, 221–37. Albuquerque: University of New Mexico Press, 1976.

Hall, Edward T. *Beyond Culture*. Garden City, NY: Doubleday, 1976.

———. *The Dance of Life: The Other Dimensions of Time*. Garden City, NY: Doubleday, 1983.

Halliday, Michael A. K. *Language as Social Semiotic: The Social Interpretation of Language and Meaning*. Baltimore: University Park Press, 1978.

Hansen, Marcus L. *The Problem of the Third Generation Immigrant*. Augustana Historical Society Publications 8. Rock Island, IL: Augustana Historical Society, 1938.

Harrill, J. Albert. *Slaves in the New Testament: Literary, Social, and Moral Dimensions*. Minneapolis: Fortress Press, 2006.

Harvey, Graham. *The True Israel: Uses of the Names Jew, Hebrew and Israel in Ancient Jewish and Early Christian Literature*. Arbeiten zur Geschichte des antiken Judentums und des Urchristentums 35. Leiden: Brill, 1996.

Herberg, Will. *Protestant-Catholic-Jew: An Essay in American Religious Sociology*. Garden City, NY: Doubleday, 1955.

Hermansen, Gustav. *Ostia: Aspects of Roman City Life*. Edmonton: University of Alberta Press, 1982.

Hofstede, Geert H. *Culture's Consequences: International Differences in Work-Related Values*. Cross-Cultural Research and Methodology Series 5. Beverly Hills, CA: Sage Publications, 1984.

———. *Culture's Consequences: Comparing Values, Behaviors, Institutions, and Organizations Across Nations*. 2nd ed. Thousand Oaks, CA: Sage Publications, 2001.

Jewett, Robert. *A Chronology of Paul's Life*. Philadelphia: Fortress Press, 1979.

Kant, Laurence H. "Jewish Inscriptions in Greek and Latin." *ANRW* II 20, 2 (1987): 617–713.

Kleinman, Arthur M. "Concepts and a Model for the Comparison of Medical Systems." In *Concepts of Health, Illness and Disease: A Comparative Perspective*, edited by Caroline Currer Meg Stacey, 29–47. New York: Berg, 1986.

Malina, Bruce J. "Christ and Time: Swiss or Mediterranean." *Catholic Biblical Quarterly* 51 (1989): 1–31. Reprinted in Bruce J. Malina. *The Social World of Jesus and the Gospels*, 179–214. New York/London: Routledge, 1996.

————. "Dealing with Biblical (Mediterranean) Characters: A Guide for U.S. Consumers." *Biblical Theology Bulletin* 19 (1989): 127–41.

————. "Is There a Circum-Mediterranean Person: Looking for Stereotypes." *Biblical Theology Bulletin* 22 (1992): 66–87.

————. *The Social Gospel of Jesus: The Kingdom of God in Mediterranean Perspective*. Minneapolis: Fortress Press, 2001.

Malina, Bruce J., and Jerome H. Neyrey. *Portraits of Paul: An Archaeology of Ancient Personality*. Louisville: Westminster/John Knox, 1996.

Malina, Bruce J., and Richard L. Rohrbaugh. *Social Science Commentary on the Synoptic Gospels*. 2nd ed. Minneapolis: Fortress Press, 2003.

Michaelis, Wilhelm. *Die Gefangenschaft des Paulus in Ephesus und das Itinerar des Timotheus. Untersuchungen zur Chronologie des Paulus und der Paulusbriefe*. Neutestamentliche Forschungen 3. Gütersloh: Bertelsmann, 1925.

Mitchell, Margaret M. "New Testament Envoys in the Context of Greco-Roman Diplomatic and Epistolary Conventions: The Example of Timothy and Titus." *Journal of Biblical Literature* 111 (1992): 641–62.

Momigliano, Arnald. *Alien Wisdom: The Limits of Hellenization*. Cambridge: Cambridge University Press, 1975.

Petrochilos, Nicholas. *Roman Attitudes to the Greeks*. S. Saripolos's Library 25. Athens: National and Capodistrian University of Athens, 1974.

Pilch, John J. "Altered States of Consciousness in the Synoptics." In *The Social Setting of Jesus and The Gospels*, edited by Wolfgang Stegemann, Bruce J. Malina, and Gerd Theissen, 103–15. Minneapolis: Fortress Press, 2002.

————. *Visions and Healings in the Acts of the Apostles: How the Early Believers Experienced God*. Collegeville, MN: Liturgical Press, 2004.

Poonawala, Ismail K. "An Ismaili Treatise on the Ijaz al-Qur'an." *Journal of the American Oriental Society* 108 (1988): 379–85.

Prickett, Stephen. *Origins of Narrative: The Romantic Appropriation of the Bible*. Cambridge/New York: Cambridge University Press, 1996.

Prior, Michael. *Paul the Letter Writer and the Second Letter to Timothy*. JSNT Supp. 23. Sheffield: JSOT Press, 1989.

Quispel, Giles. "The *Asclepius*: From the Hermetic Lodge in Alexandria to the Greek Eucharist and the Roman Mass." In *Gnosis and Hermeticism from Antiquity to Modern Times*, edited by Roelof van den Broek and Wouter J. Hanegraaff, 69–78. Albany: SUNY Press, 1998.

Rogers, Everett M. *Diffusion of Innovations*. 4th ed. New York: Free Press, 1995.

Rogers, Everett M., with F. Floyd Shoemaker. *Communication of Innovations: A Cross-Cultural Approach*. 2nd ed. New York: Free Press, 1971.

Rogers, Everett M., with Lynne Svenning. *Modernization Among Peasants: The Impact of Communication*. New York: Holt, Rinehart and Winston, 1969.

Rohrbaugh, Richard L. "Gossip in the New Testament." In *Social Science Models for Interpreting the Bible: Essays by the Context Group in Honor of Bruce J. Malina*, edited by John J. Pilch, 239–59. Biblical Interpretation Series 53. Leiden: Brill, 2001.

———. "Ethnocentrism and the Historical Questions About Jesus." In *The Social Setting of Jesus and the Gospels*, edited by Wolfgang Stegemann, Bruce J. Malina, and Gerd Theissen, 27–44. Minneapolis: Fortress Press, 2002.

Rubin, N. "Mšykt 'wrlh wtqnt hpry'h [On Drawing Down the Prepuce and Incision of the Foreskin—Peri'ah])." *Zion* (Jerusalem) 54, no. 1 (1989): 105–17.

Sumner, William G. *Folkways: A Study of the Sociological Importance of Usages, Manners, Customs, Mores, and Morals*. Boston: Ginn, 1906.

Talbert, Charles H. *Literary Patterns, Theological Themes, and the Genre of Luke-Acts*. Cambridge, MA: Society of Biblical Literature 20; Missoula, MT: distributed by Scholars' Press [1975] c. 1974.

Trevijano Etcheverría, Ramón. "Los Viajes de Timoteo y la secuencia de las cartas paulinas." *Estudios Bíblicos* 57 (1999): 683–709.

Triandis, Harry C. "Cross-Cultural Studies in Individualism and Collectivism." In *Nebraska Symposium on Motivation 1989*, edited by R. A. Diensbier and J. J. Berman, 41–133. Lincoln: University of Nebraska Press, 1990.

———. *Individualism and Collectivism*. New Directions in Social Psychology. San Francisco: Westview Press, 1995.

Veyne, Paul. "*Humanitas*: Romans and Non-Romans." In *The Romans*, edited by Andrea Giardina. Translated by Lydia G. Cochrane, 342–69. Chicago: University of Chicago Press, 1993.

Walbank, F. W. "The Problem of Greek Nationality." In *Greeks and Barbarians*, edited by Thomas Harrison, 234–56. New York: Routledge, 2002.

White, Hayden. *Metahistory: The Historical Imagination in Nineteenth Century Europe*. Baltimore: Johns Hopkins University Press, 1973.

SCRIPTURE AND ANCIENT
AUTHORS INDEX

INDEX OF PERSONS AND SUBJECTS